Mercy on the Trail

(Book #2 in *Mercy Trilogy*)

Sheri McLaughlin

Mercy on the Trail

More Books by Sheri McLaughlin:

*Presidential Mercy**

Angry Hornets

Terror Unleashed: Angry Hornets Return

Lovers Fall in Arcticville

Frozen Isolation

A New Adventure on the Escuadrón Polar

Whispering Angels

Vanishing Author

*First book in the *Mercy Trilogy*

Table of Contents

Author's Disclaimer/Notes

Mercy on the Trail has been simmering on the back burner for a while. Actual events in history were tweaked and embellished to contribute to a believable plot line. It is pure fiction. Character names and corporation titles are fabricated. If there are any semblances to actual persons, beings, places, occurrences, or circumstances, it is strictly coincidental. None of the material in this book is meant to harm or sway anyone toward or against any person, group, or political party. I only hope to provide entertainment. The descriptions, views, ideas, and/or opinions expressed are those belonging to me, the author, and do not reflect the official policy or position of any religion, group, politician, or elected official. It is not my intent to malign any creature, religion, ethnic group, club, organization, company, individual, anyone, or anything.

Also, I am fully aware that the traditional underground coal mines have been shut down and replaced with open mines. For the sole purpose of aiding in the plot, I have chosen to keep an active traditional coal mine. Hobet in West Virginia was the deepest coal mine. It was in operation for 41 years.

Chapter 1 - Turmoil in Kabul

In the wee hours of the morning, Taliban fighters quickly gained a foothold in Kabul. After capturing military equipment worth millions of dollars that was meant for Afghan forces, it didn't take long for militants to acquire armored vehicles, Black Hawk helicopters, and military weapons.

Threatening the Afghan people to conform, Humvees were positioned by Taliban forces to block every major escape route leading in and out of Kabul. Explosions were detonated near sites previously occupied by Americans, including the US Embassy. The free world had been sent a clear message - *get out and stay out.*

The Taliban specifically targeted Afghans who helped the US military. When news spread that the enemy acquired sophisticated biometric devices used by the US military to identify Afghan allies, they had no choice but to either escape or hide below ground in caves or tunnels.

Afghans, who agreed to be interviewed, hid their faces before conveying to BBC reporters that they never expected the hasty takeover. Two older women feared their rights would once again be abolished under Taliban rule.

*****

Prior military experience did not lessen the horror President Robin Langford felt as she watched the events unfold hour by hour. In the Situation Room, Robin learned there might not be enough time to evacuate everyone.

President Langford sighed. "This is a disaster! They knew the invasion was imminent, which was why our guys spent the last six months urging people to evacuate!"

General George Whitlock interrupted, "Madam President, intelligence and military sources on the ground are reporting another vicious attack in Kabul."

President Langford shook her head in disbelief as she listened to the horrific details. Agitated, she watched helplessly as heartbreaking developments unfolded. Demanding answers, she slammed her fist against the top of a large oblong table and shouted in frustration, "They've been training with us for twenty years! The Afghan military is not fighting back! Don't they want to preserve a better way of life?"

Vice President Bill Harper, the Joint Chiefs of Staff, and General Whitlock were fully aware that the exit strategy was hardly a last minute decision. It took the military heads over two years to plan.

Robin clasped her hands together, pressing her forehead against perpendicular thumbs. Shoulder-length mocha locks brushed against her wrists as she closed her eyes, tears streamed down her gaunt cheeks when she remembered her husband lovingly squeezing her shoulders. It was his way of offering support after she told him about the exit strategy.

Little did Robin know, three months later, her husband would collapse and die suddenly from a blood clot in the brain. Prior to his death, Gerry Langford managed to live with the effects of Parkinson's disease with hardly any complaints.

President Robin Langford abstained from taking pain medications, if she could help it. Multiple surgeries to remove shrapnel meant dealing with aches and pains daily. One particular pain, however, was permeating her thoughts. The additional stress contributed to a splitting migraine headache.

Excusing herself, she needed to take a break. She exited the room and rushed back to the Oval Office, hoping to stop the pounding before nausea set in. *Ugh! The last time my head felt like this was when I woke up from surgery after being shot!*

Swallowing the pills in unison, she chased them down with a cold bottle of water. She shivered, as the waves of regret washed over her. She couldn't stop the flow of tears, trying to conceal them with a tissue. *Gerry, I wish you were here right now. I could use your support.*

Making her way back to the Situation Room, she paused to view a small television located in the break room. It was broadcasting the news on a more conservative network. Despite her Green Party affiliation, the media accused her of copying her husband's liberal agenda. *Wow, how quickly they forget I've often sided with conservative platforms.*

Despite the turmoil Robin faced during her Presidency, she effectively managed to run the country, suppressing her feelings in the public eye. The pain she endured from her AR15 injuries paled in comparison to the heartache she was experiencing from losing her soul mate. Some days, she just barely managed to drag herself out of bed in the morning.

The media had been critiquing Robin's weight loss. Rumors were spreading and one far right news station was quoted saying, 'She was sicker than the President lead the public to believe.' Another news tabloid falsely reported she was dying of cancer.

Republicans were lining up to sweep the next election by casting doubts and issuing political backlash propaganda against the Democrats. Bradley Juniper was the favored Republican candidate. He was running against Kelly Farrah, a fierce liberal Democrat.

President Langford did not usually conform to any particular party, but she was adamantly opposed to Farrah's extreme political antics. Crossing her arms, President Langford shook her head in disgust as she listened to more personal attacks against her. *Clearly, this is trash-worthy news at its finest!*

*****

News broadcasts covered the chaos just outside the Kabul Airport. In a crowded street, Afghan survivors scrambled to vacate their homeland.

Barbed wire loops had been strewn along the top of a concrete barrier just outside Kabul's military airport. A hasty decision was made to cut away sections of the razor sharp deterrent to permit emergency accessibility into the airport. Frightened Afghan men, women, and children were using all of their might to push forward. Another barricade was forced open. A wave of people funneled through the narrow gap hoping to flee oppressive Taliban forces.

An armored vehicle swerved wildly on the sandy terrain, stopping just short of the mob. A dark-haired, bearded man with tan leathery skin braced a machine gun underneath his armpit. He stood on top of the vehicle inside a rooftop cage mounted at the rear. In Arabic, his deep voice shouted, "Get back! Get back!" He was not a member of the US military even though he wore Army combat clothing that had been found in an abandoned barrack just outside of Kabul. Angrily squawking, he squinted into the direction of the hot sun, haphazardly firing one round overhead the anxious crowd.

Shrill voices echoed amidst the smoke filled, dusty air.

With only six thousand US troops left on the ground, surrounded by a fully armed Taliban army; it was all the military could do to perform their assigned duties. The ultimate goal was to evacuate Americans and allies, saving them from a sour predicament.

Reporters on the ground continued to cover the madness, broadcasting about an angry throng of desperate people trying to escape Taliban infested areas. Day and night, C-17 military planes flew in and out of Kabul's Airport. Overloaded planes were being sent to Qatar, Germany, and select military bases all over the world.

*****

Isaad and Emma Dil were sandwiching their son, Taji, between them. Slowly edging closer to the airport, Isaad knew he was on the Taliban's hit list. Assisting American soldiers over the last eighteen years, Isaad needed to keep a low profile.

Meanwhile, Abdul, another Taliban soldier monitoring the push, made an impromptu decision to flee Afghanistan. Squirming his short, lean body through the crowd, Abdul noticed a small family. He positioned himself behind the child and pointed a loaded pistol at Taji's right temple. "Tell them I am your brother or the boy dies."

They were nearing a checkpoint operated by members of the United States Marines.

Isaad and Emma exchanged worrisome glances. Agreeing to lie to protect their child was their only option. They hoped the weapon this evil man was holding would be discovered and confiscated. They watched the man slide the weapon into a hidden holster underneath a baggy pant leg.

Jackson Troy, a soldier in the US Marines, recognized his friend. He spoke in Farsi. "Isaad, I'm so glad you made it!"

Isaad tried not to act nervous. "Jackson! Meet my family, this is my son, Taji; my wife, Emma; and my brother…" He cleared his voice.

Filling in the awkward pause, he replied, "Hi, I'm Abdul…"

Jackson added Abdul's name to his list, automatically giving him the last name, Dil. After he shook hands with everyone, he patted Isaad on the back. Then he commented. "Isaad, I didn't realize you had a brother."

Isaad looked down at his son. "Yes, well, it's a long story. Forgive and forget, that's what I always say. The difficult times are what makes us realize what's important in life."

"Yes, indeed…" Jackson pointed his right index finger over Emma's head. "Okay, you see that crowd of people surrounding that C-17 aircraft?"

"Yes, I see it." Isaad held his hand up to shield his eyes from the sun. He swallowed, tasting the bitter dusty air.

"That's the last flight today, weather forecasts are warning us about an approaching dust storm. We're going to have to cram as many people in there as we can. Good luck, my friend…" Jackson shook Isaad's hand again and waved goodbye.

After uncomfortably stacking people in the C-17 aircraft, it took off about a half hour later. The refugees would eventually end up at Langley Air Force Base in Virginia.

*****

Just outside of the evacuation point in Kabul, members of Isis-K disagreed with the way the Taliban was handling the situation. Determined to open up the roads and kill anyone in the way, a short chunky man wearing lightweight Pashtun clothing inserted himself among a dense crowd of people who were hoping to gain entry into the airport.

Seconds later, a loud explosion sent many to an early grave. The suicide bomber perished after completing his mission. Bloodied, mutilated bodies were laying motionless on the ground. Twenty American soldiers were among the dead. They had been situated just outside of the airport enclosure to assist in streamlining the evacuation process.

"Jackson! Jackson, no!" Peter ran toward his military buddy. He saw Jackson laying still, eyes open in a pool of blood, partially exposed organs. "Please don't die on me here. Not now!"

Three Afghan minors were crying out in fear and anger, clinging to nearby witnesses for support. In an instant, several children became orphans. The horrific images replayed in their young, impressionable minds. Looking for answers to the questions: *What happens now? Where will we go?*

Two Afghan mothers kneeled and cradled their deceased children in their arms. Rocking and loudly weeping, one of the women removed her hijab and wrapped it underneath her son's skull in an ill attempt at controlling the massive hemorrhaging. This removal of her head covering was considered an abomination of the strict dress code honored by extremists like Isis-K and the Taliban.

Meanwhile, a Taliban soldier pointed his weapon at the women and shouted orders in his native tongue, "Move, get out of the way!" When neither of the women budged, he forcefully grabbed the woman without a head covering by the hair and dragged her into the middle of the street. He struck her multiple times with the blunt end of a weapon and kicked her in the gut. Curled up in agonizing pain, she sobbed inconsolably. Her clothing was wet, soaked with her son's blood.

Both Taliban and Isis-K used extreme demonstrative force to make others comply. It was one of the reasons many chose to flee.

American troops in the vicinity arrived at the scene of the explosion to retrieve the bodies of their fallen comrades. Alicia, a fully armed first class private marine, approached the injured, grieving Afghan woman and helped her up. When she learned about another grieving mother and the young fatalities, Alicia comforted them and offered her assistance.

The women were still in shock, so Alicia used a military grade walkie-talkie to request medical assistance. Moments later, stretchers arrived to move the bodies off the street. She reassured the mothers that reverent care would be provided.

The evacuation process grounded to a halt when a spiraling dust storm struck Kabul. Everyone covered their faces and sought shelter inside nearby buildings. Civil order was maintained, at least for a short time.

The following day, more airplanes returned to Kabul Airport to resume evacuations after clearing the sand-clogged runways. New orders were received requiring all planes to fire flares during takeoffs. This was a method used to deter being fired upon by rogue militants.

*****

Four hours later, President Langford returned to the Oval Office. She reviewed the speech that had been prepared for her. It was her duty to brief American citizens about the latest developments in Afghanistan.

Elizabeth Hoover, Secretary of Defense, interrupted. "Madam President, we're getting reports of gun shots and a bomb. Multiple casualties, including members of our military…"

"Elizabeth, I want to talk to the head of the Taliban, NOW! They promised us two weeks! Shit, this cannot be happening!" President Langford was beyond livid.

*****

Processing paperwork took too much time. United States military planes carried hoards of refugees out to ally bases around the world. Despite being uncomfortably packed in, like sardines, those on board the flights were considered the lucky ones.

A conservative news channel was covering the latest developments in the evacuation process. One news station, in particular, broadcasted live from Qatar. Anchorman Gary Delta asked, "Amy, we are hearing reports about Afghans fleeing without the proper paperwork. Are you getting any feedback from your sources that would confirm this?"

Amy replied, "Yes, Gary. Military folks on the front lines have recently shared their concerns about the evacuation process, saying there has not been enough time to run the proper checks."

*****

Deborah Wooly, Secretary of Homeland Security, had been watching the latest news reports out of Qatar. She immediately contacted the President. "Madam President, we need to discuss our Nation's security!"

Ten minutes later, Deborah was pacing in the President's Oval Office.

Deborah's voice rose, "Madam President, we need to sort through the incoming refugees to verify their identities. How will we accurately determine friend from foe? This could potentially become a horrible situation. Don't forget 9-11! We could be playing right into a terrorist's hands!"

President Langford's attempts to reassure Deborah fell on deaf ears. With a surge of refugees arriving on US soil at an unprecedented rate, the Secretary of Homeland Security made a valid point. Military personnel was overwhelmed and understaffed. The interrogation process was tedious.

The door to the Oval Office opened and Elizabeth Hoover poked her head in. "Madam President, Hazrat Aryo is on Line 3."

President Langford purposely spoke in front of the Defense Secretary. "Would you please excuse me, Deborah. I need to take this call." Elizabeth Hoover opened the door wider for Ms. Wooly to exit so President Langford could speak in private with the head of the Taliban.

Deborah Wooly's face reddened and she let out a sigh, storming out of the Oval Office.

President Langford pressed the blinking button and spoke. "Hazrat, you promised to give the United States two weeks to evacuate! Why is the Taliban attacking?"

Hazrat answered, "Madam President, those were isolated attacks from members of Isis-K. The Taliban has already taken care of the matter. I assure you, we will not tolerate Isis-K interfering with our agreement."

US government officials and military leaders issued stern public warnings to Isis-K members, threatening retaliation for any further demonstrations in Kabul. It was obvious tensions in Afghanistan were becoming more volatile. Avoiding conflict and protecting the evacuees were Langford's main priorities.

*****

President Langford called her military advisors back into her office. "The Taliban has assured me this was an isolated incident from Isis-K. I'm going to ask for assistance from our allies to help us meet the evacuation deadline."

Deborah Wooly, Secretary of Homeland Security, spontaneously returned to the Oval Office. She had been determined to get in the last word. Impatiently interrupting, "With all due respect, Madam President, the evacuation process is happening too quickly! I do not believe we have enough military manpower to handle the necessary checks on undocumented Afghans entering the United States!"

President Robin Langford sat forward in her executive chair with her arms crossed and defended her position. She did not appreciate Wooly's pretentious interruption. "Look, I trust our military is handling the situation in the best possible way. The Secretary of Defense has assured me our military has been following proper protocols before anyone is released into the United States."

Deborah clenched her hands and displayed an angry scowl. She pressed one hand over her eyes and whispered under her breath, "God, help us all." Then she exited as quickly as she'd arrived.

*****

Omar and Skid went to school together in Kabul, learning the Pashto language and Farsi. After graduation, Omar studied English and worked in the construction business while Skid worked at a medical supplies company.

Omar Qurban befriended Skid Nuri shortly after Skid found his parents dead. Skid refused to believe their deaths were caused by opium overdoses. He always suspected the Taliban had a hand in it, since his father worked alongside the United States military.

Omar and Skid were separated after landing in Qatar. Omar arrived at a military base in

Virginia, while Skid's plane went to a military base in San Antonio, Texas.

Randolph Air Force Base

Sitting quietly on one of the metal folding chairs, Skid closely studied the behaviors and mannerisms of the Americans. Running his left hand along his beard to smooth it down, he preferred to speak either Pashto or Farsi. He only spoke a little English.

Rodney, an American soldier, was dressed in a combat uniform. When Skid approached the soldier, he was initially greeted in English. Skid nodded. He tried replying in broken English. "No, no passport… Here take…" Skid held his work identification badge with his photo. He gave a friendly smile, yielding few teeth. Rodney decided it was best to repeat the questioning in Farsi.

Skid shook his head. In Farsi, he responded, "The Taliban took everything from me. I have nothing."

Soon after receiving a temporary visa, he sought employment at a local shipyard near San Antonio. He did not have much money, so it would be impossible for him to travel to Virginia at this time. He promised himself he'd travel to Virginia one day to reconnect with his pal, Omar.

Langley Air Force Base

Omar faced similar interrogations by US military personnel. He chose to reply in English. "The Taliban took my passport."

Since both Skid and Omar did not have the proper paperwork, they were each granted humanitarian parole which allowed them to enter the United States for a temporary period of time.

*****

Back in Kabul, 16-year old Alibaba (Ali) Finjaven was one of the few kids who attended school during this uncertain time in Kabul. Ali's father told him today would be his last; they would be leaving Afghanistan tonight.

Ali knew it would be the last time he'd see his best friend, Ikram. They always walked home from school together. Ali's best bud lived next door.

"I'll be right back. I just need to ask Mom what time we are leaving." Ali plopped his backpack down at his buddy's house so they could play a video game, as promised.

Ali thought it was strange that the front door was unlocked. He opened the door and walked toward the kitchen. "Hello! Where is everybody?"

It was unusual that his mother wasn't right there to greet him. But then he figured she's probably packing.

He made his way to the kitchen to grab a soda. "Mom! What time are we...?" He stopped short when he discovered his mother and Anqa, his little sister, lying in a pool of blood. Their faces were ghostly white.

Ali screamed and fled in despair. Returning to Ikram's home, fear caused him to hold off texting his dad. The overwhelming shock of seeing his mom and sister clouded his thinking.

Ikram didn't know how to console his friend. But he told Ali about a tunnel underneath his house. "We can hide there until my parents get home."

Ali suddenly remembered something. He carried a fake passport in his backpack. His father had obtained fake passports for the entire family to avoid being targeted by the Taliban, but Ali knew something must have gone wrong.

"Okay, let me just grab my backpack." The dates on the fake passport aged Ali by several years. This also allowed him to work part time so he could earn extra money for his family.

Aware of what the Taliban was capable of, Ali did not have time to grieve. He needed to pull himself together and keep the promises he made to his father.

Ali's father taught him how to send coded messages in the Pashto language. *Power grid* meant the family unit. Most of the time, Ali's text messages would just say, 'Power grid okay.' This would let his dad know everyone was home safe.

This message would be different, "Power grid out." Ali did not know that his father was being detained by Taliban fighters.

One of the Taliban interrogators grabbed the phone that had been taken from the detainee when the screen lit up with a new message. The text didn't make any sense to the interrogator. He scratched his head, clearly confused. Then he confronted Rammi about it.

Rammi just shrugged it off as no big deal, camouflaging his pain. Previously working as a translator to help US troops, he was determined to keep his true identity private. The fake passport completed the disguise.

Fortunately, the Taliban believed Rammi's story about working in the opium fields and released him later that afternoon. They handed the passport and phone back, gruffly waving him off.

*****

Rammi knew where to find Ali. He knocked on the neighbor's door.

Ikram's father had a rifle in his hands and looked through the peephole. He immediately opened the door and invited Rammi inside. "Rammi, Ali is with Ikram. Follow me."

Rammi was shown the underground passageway where the boys had been hiding underneath two large floor tiles.

*****

Ikram and his father accompanied Rammi and Ali, waiting in a large crowd of evacuees. They were the last ones to board the flight to Qatar, feeling lucky they were among the fortunate to leave Afghanistan behind.

Rammi and Ali would be the first ones on board the flight to a military base in Texas. After intense questioning, they were released into the United States.

Rammi's experience assisting the military by repairing various modes of transportation helped him gain employment at El Paso International Airport. He was one of the lucky to obtain such a prestigious job, given mechanics were in high demand.

Chapter 2 – Mexican Border

Venezuelans were being driven out of their home country by a ruthless dictatorship. Without having the means to fight back, Delgado and Ramon left their families behind to gain access to the United States. Joining a group of fellow Venezuelans, they pooled resources together for the long journey, encountering many hardships along the way. Relying on the kindness of perfect strangers for food and shelter became the norm.

Dangerous situations were unavoidable, given the hazardous conditions. Death was not uncommon. Simply marked grave sites were gruesome reminders of what could go wrong.

*****

In Reynosa, one Mexican drug lord lived well, running illegal trafficking operations across the southern border of the United States. Everyone called this man, Araña Malvado, which, in Spanish, means Evil Spider.

Araña lived in a heavily guarded trailer. He had a wide network of followers who understood never to disagree with Malvado. Everyone was aware he murdered his own brother to take charge of the lucrative operation.

*****

Arrangements had been made in advance with Araña, who was also the leader of the largest Mexican drug cartel south of the Rio Grande.

Delgado and Ramon prepaid handsomely for two loaded handguns to take across the United States border. The guns would only be used for protection.

The sun set hours before the group approached the compound. Bright lights illuminated the complex in the distance. The weary group pressed on until they bumped into one of Araña's men.

After submitting a large sum of cash, the group was given a map of the deep tunnel system. Wasting no time, an armed guard lifted the hinged wooden door and motioned each inside, one by one.

Ramon and Delgado intentionally lingered behind, distancing themselves from the group they'd walked over 2,000 miles with. Once it was just the two of them, Ramon signaled to the man holding the trap door. They spoke quietly, explaining the agreement.

Nodding his head, the man walked away and entered a well-lit double wide trailer.

Moments later, Araña Malvado ducked his head as he exited the trailer and sternly waved at the men from afar. Under the porch lighting, Malvado paused to flick the top portion of a cigarette off the bottom of his shoe. The tall, thin man with a scruffy beard nodded his head and smirked when the guard handed him the bag of cash. Malvado walked toward the pair and stopped to assess the situation. He stared through them with deadpan eyes. Squinting, he brought the smoking item to his lips and took a long drag before exhaling a cloud of smoke.

The smoke made Ramon cough. He was feeling extremely nervous. In Spanish, Ramon spoke. "Hello, sir, I'm Ramon and this is Delgado. We wired you an extra $2,000.00 for two hand guns in addition to secret access into the United States."

"Of course, but it is unfortunate that the price has increased. It will be two thousand dollars more!" The tall bearded man was now pointing his pistol at them. Clearly, he was not in the mood to negotiate.

It was late at night and Delgado and Ramon were stuck in Reynosa, relying on assistance from a vicious drug lord. Araña sensed the men were desperate enough to pay more.

Delgado protested, "But that wasn't what we agreed to. We don't have that kind of money on us. Besides, we've already paid you plenty!"

Araña's lifeless eyes narrowed. He lifted his pistol and fired several shots into Delgado's chest cavity.

Ramon stepped back, helplessly watching, mouth gaping wide, as his friend collapsed face down in a pool of blood. Without hesitation, Ramon handed over his entire wallet with all of his cash, knowing it was only $1,751.00. A few hundred bucks short of the new demand. Beads of sweat were forming on his face. He closed his eyes and prayed it would be enough to preserve his life.

The Evil Spider bent down and reached for the wallet in the dead man's back pocket. After retrieval, he looked up at Ramon. "If you want to live, you'll do what I say."

After almost soiling his pants, Ramon opened one eye to look back at Araña. Ramon had been backed into a corner. Fearing he would end up like his friend, Ramon agreed to Araña's terms.

Araña motioned to another guard who was holding an AK-47. Ramon watched him whisper something in the man's ear. Then the guard grabbed Ramon by the biceps and shoved him into a sterile empty room, well lit with white walls and one chair. Ramon's photograph was taken and he was left alone for at least another hour or so.

Araña returned to brief Ramon about expectations. Ramon was handed a genuine looking US passport using his actual name, Ramon Blanco. "Don't lose this! You'll need it."

Then Ramon's wallet was tossed into his lap. "This should keep you going for a little while."

Araña handed him another cell phone which contained an image of Ramon's family on the home screen. It was to ensure people, like Ramon, understood the consequences. "Only use this to communicate with me. When I call, you answer. If you double cross me, you and your family die! It's as simple as that."

Another guard entered the room holding a backpack that contained a cell phone charger, two large water bottles, detailed maps of the tunnel system, a flashlight with extra batteries, and one locked and loaded untraceable handgun.

Ramon followed the guard out to the trap door and descended into the dark abyss underground. He flipped the switch on the flashlight and proceeded to make his way through the tunnel.

This elaborate tunnel system ran between Mexico and Texas, underneath the Rio Grande. Many of Malvado's men died digging these tunnels which were over 61 feet deep. Construction of the tunnels was treacherous, but no one would ever dare to refuse orders from Malvado.

The stale air mixed with the stench of human waste made Ramon feel nauseous. Images of the bloody scene played back in his mind and propelled him to keep moving.

The map directed him to the right at an underground fork. It was the only way he could really go since the other tunnel had been boarded up. This tunnel looked newer, but it was a smaller tube, so he needed to crawl another 3,000 feet to the very end. Ramon stood up again, once the space dead ended. He noticed a wooden ladder attached to the far wall. Using his only source of light, he pointed it at the ladder. Then he reached up with his free hand and climbed, using his other elbow to help stabilize.

Lifting the wooden hinged door, he assumed he was somewhere in the United States. Brushing the dirt off his trousers, Ramon used the flashlight to examine his new surroundings. It looked like an abandoned mine of some kind. There was an old hardhat covered in dirt and graffiti written in English on the walls. Pushing against the boarded up mine shaft, he realized it wasn't going to budge. *This can't be right! There's no way a person could fit through here.*

His head turned around and he re-aimed the flashlight. The cool musty darkness groaned. *What is that noise?*

He reexamined the maps and realized there might be another way to exit the mine. He listened to the eerie howls, as winds swirled through gaps in the cave. *Whoosh!*

*****

Ramon felt his heart racing. After the lengthy delay, finding an exit was a top priority. The last thing he wanted was to be caught by US border patrol agents, even though he had a passport. At the very least, his presence out here would raise too many suspicions. Daylight was his nemesis; he needed to remain hidden.

"Owww!"

*****

The border town of Mission, Texas had a pink glow at the crack of dawn. Traffic was light, but the illuminated Walmart sign acted like a beacon.

Ramon didn't notice anyone in the vicinity. His focus was on his big toe that was swelling inside his shoe. It throbbed after stubbing it against a stalagmite on the floor of the cave.

He limped toward the big box store which didn't open until 6 a.m. He still had over a half hour. *Shit!*

Hobbling over to a Holiday Inn Express over two miles away, he entered the lobby.

*****

The desk clerk was just finishing the night shift. He stared at the gentleman with a backpack. "Hello. Welcome to the Holiday Inn Express." It was the standard greeting.

Breathing heavy, the man pulled out his wallet and asked in broken English, "Need one room please."

The clerk scrunched his nose when he sensed a foul odor. This man's appearance confirmed he probably hadn't showered in a while. He punched the information into the computer. "The cheapest available room will cost $135.72 per night. That price includes taxes and service fees. Breakfast is included."

To the clerk's surprise, Ramon pulled out a wad of cash and handed it to the clerk. "Three nights please."

Across the street, Ramon ignored the stares and limped into the big box discount store. He purchased basic hygiene products, one pair of pants, two collared shirts, socks, men's briefs, and a box of bandages. When he returned to his room, the shower was more than refreshing, it was a necessary step in returning to humanity.

Ramon was aware that his money would not last long here. He needed to find a job quickly.

Chapter 3 – Rammi and Ali

Almost one year after Rammi and Ali escaped Afghanistan, they settled in a small two-story home in Mission, Texas. His father learned most of his English while working on the job. He oftentimes spoke Farsi with Ali, unless they were out in public.

Ali attended high school. After school, he often collected the mail before unlocking the door. Setting his backpack down, he respectfully greeted his father in his native tongue. "Good day, papa…"

Late in his junior year, Ali took additional classes to learn English. Ali was actually three years younger than his peers. At the age of 13, it was just easier to avoid lengthy explanations. Ali was intelligent, but his smaller stature and pre-pubescent voice made him an easy target for bullies. It was difficult, at times, to fit in. His upbringing taught him to be resilient and strong. Soon he would make friends and overcome social hurdles, excelling in most of his subjects, especially advanced math classes.

He applied at various colleges in Texas to help keep tuition costs manageable. After opening an envelope addressed to him, he couldn't wait to share the good news.

*****

Ali paused to grin as he witnessed his father's comical interactions with American television. Rammi was extremely opinionated and wildly gestured, as he shook his head in disbelief.

Ali overheard the news depicting poor Americans in need of government assistance. He watched his dad raise a fist in protest.

His father remarked, "Would you look at this guy! That's an expensive iPhone he's holding. Americans don't know what poor is. Disgraceful!"

Ali smirked and rhetorically noted, "Just imagine if they had to live under the Taliban's rules, Papa."

Rammi chuckled and coughed, "True! I am doubtful Americans understand the meaning of hardship."

Ali decided to change the subject, "Dad, I have good news! I've been accepted in the pharmacy department at Texas A & M! And they have offered me a full scholarship."

Rammi jumped out of his recliner and waved both arms into the air. "Ali! You did? Aaah, amazing! I'm so proud of you. We celebrate your successes tonight." He walked over to a small cookie jar and lifted the lid. Ruffling through the papers, he pinched one large restaurant coupon and lifted it up to double check the expiration date. "Here, two for the price of one at *Under One Roof*!" The local diner was well known for a variety of dishes and routinely served large portions.

"Sure, Dad! That sounds good."

*****

After dinner, Rammi and Ali stopped by the market to pick up a half gallon of milk.

Noticing a young man digging through a trash can, Rammi took pity on him. "Young man! Excuse me, what is your name? Where are you from?"

Cautiously offering a wave, "Uh, Ramon from Venezuela…"

Rammi was curious about this young man. "Ramon, where do you live now?"

Ramon looked down at the ground, feeling ashamed. Then he pointed his index finger at a set of dumpsters where a tattered quilt had been neatly folded. A backpack sat on top. He'd chosen this location to block the cool desert breezes at night.

Rammi had an unfamiliar accent. "Ramon, I give you proposition. You stay with us in basement." He turned to his son for help.

Rammi spoke to his son, Ali, in his native tongue, asking him to help translate the specific details for him.

Ali nodded his head and turned to look at Ramon. "My papa has three conditions. First, you find a job. Second, no smoking or drugs and, third, no wild parties."

Ramon studied their mannerisms, he was hesitant to believe people could be this kind. "I dunno… What's the catch?"

Again, Ali translated, "We come from Afghanistan. Papa believes in hard work and second chances."

Ramon smiled and nodded his head. "Okay, deal." Ramon shook both Rammi's and Ali's hands. Then he hoisted his backpack onto one shoulder and followed them home.

Chapter 4 – Campaign Promises

Bart Gowkoni, President Langford's driven campaign manager, was also a sharp dresser. He wore designer suits and his dark hair was slicked back. A lampshade-style mustache finished the look. Friends often teased him about looking like a gangster.

Bart scheduled a rally to conjure up support in the upcoming election. He was dedicated, relentlessly working to persuade others to join the Green Party's independent caucus. He devoted most of his free time to budgeting and fundraising. Enlisting the help of Melody and Peggy Langford, the trio reminded the public about the President's many positive values and strengths.

Unfortunately, stress caused Bart to begin smoking again. At first, it was just a few cigs here and there. He'd hide the packs in his desk at work and try to camouflage the odor with breath mints and air fresheners.

One day, Bart's life partner of seven years noticed a foul smell on his clothing. He gave

Bart an ultimatum to quit or else. Bart knew what that meant, but he could not give up the habit. It cost him his relationship.

*****

For the past ten months, Melody and Peggy put their own ambitions on hold to assist with their mother's campaign, making thousands of phone calls to help raise over 200 million dollars. Team Langford refused to give up, despite negative remarks on several news channels.

With significant decline in Presidential approval ratings since the tragic Afghanistan pullout, Robin's campaign promises fell by the wayside. The economy plunged into a deep recession. Her ratings plummeted and the scuttlebutt around town was that either a Democrat or a Republican would win the ticket.

Congress's divided interests made it all the more difficult for Robin to fulfill what she set out to accomplish. Although her hands were oftentimes tied, she had great love for her country. She especially hated to see it divided.

If constant negative feedback about her dwindling popularity weren't disheartening enough, Robin was dealing with return trips to the hospital. Those visits were a constant reminder of the attempt on her life almost four years ago.

The most recent surgery was necessary to remove a small shrapnel-induced tumor on Robin's right lung. Embedded fragments of tungsten alloy caused a rare, yet small pulmonary rhabdomyosarcoma. Past checkups never revealed this mass. Doctors expressed how fortunate she was that the tumor had been discovered early.

Fortunate wasn't how Robin saw her situation. Yes, she was alive, but far from thriving, especially after losing her husband. Some days it seemed like she was barely hanging on. Her daughters were the sole reason she was keeping her sanity through it all.

Robin's PTSD symptoms included agonizing bouts of depression and anxiety. It seemed impossible to stop the looping thoughts which resulted in a short fuse and jumpiness whenever she heard a loud noise. But as long as she was the Commander in Chief, she'd need to keep the diagnosis under her hat. The public, as well as her family, could never know that she was suffering with this condition. Keeping silent meant she'd have to weather it alone.

She shifted her primary focus on the needs of the United States. Preoccupation helped suppress her feelings. She set up an emergency staff meeting to strategize on ways to reboot the economy without harming the environment in the process. Whether or not she could counteract the country's dismal financial status, public opinion remained the same, blaming her for it all.

*****

A surge in job losses added to the spiraling recession which forced an uptick in foreclosures. In 48 hours, the S & P plunged another 200 points. With Congress at an impasse, the Nation's public healthcare system was in danger of crumbling once again.

*****

Four months prior to the election, Peggy and Melody Langford looked sharp, standing in the Oval Office wearing similar navy blue skirts and complimenting silk blouses.

Waiting for Bart Gowkoni to arrive, the girls sat down next to each other on a Victorian upholstered couch. Bart entered two minutes later. He formally greeted the President.

Folding her bony hands on top of the desk, Robin Langford leaned forward and smiled. "Good afternoon, Bart! Please, have a seat."

The campaign was running smoothly; donations were pouring in. They were expecting to get a pat on the back for their hard work.

As usual, Bart sat with his legs crossed in one of the adjacent stately chairs. His shiny loafers reflected the light as he adjusted his polka dotted tie in anticipation.

President Langford cleared her voice before speaking. "I imagine you'd like to know why I called this meeting. First and foremost, I appreciate the work you all have been putting into my campaign. It has meant the world to me."

"Happy to do it, Madam President." Bart beamed.

Melody and Peggy exchanged glances and swallowed hard. Seeing the dark circles under their mother's eyes, they sensed she was under tremendous pain and pressure. Ever since their father passed, mom hadn't been the same. It was like watching all of the life she once had slowly drain out of her. They hoped the successful campaign contribution numbers would cheer her up.

Robin paused to take a sip of water. "I think it'd be best if I abandon my campaign for reelection. I decided to support Bradley Juniper, the Republican nominee."

The Langford sisters stood up in unison. Peggy spoke with emotion in her voice, "Are you sure that's what YOU want to do? We just want you to be happy."

Melody scrunched her nose, "But I don't understand. I thought you were against the Republicans because of the fracking. You know, Dad really hated fracking."

Robin nodded in reply, "The country has been struggling and they deserve better than what I've been able to give them. I will always love your Dad and everything he stood for. I hope you realize that. Look, Bradley is a straight shooter. He is the most liberal conservative I have ever met. Kelly Farrah is just too far left. Quite frankly, she scares me."

"Are you really sure you want to do this, Madam President? I believe you have a good chance of winning." Bart remained hopeful she might change her mind. His even-keeled temperament hid his deep disappointment.

"Bart, you have done an amazing job. I will be sure to give you stellar recommendations." President Langford knew, without a doubt, this was the right decision for her.

Chapter 5 – Bradley Juniper

Born and raised in Atlanta, Georgia, Bradley Juniper, was an African American journeyman who worked to pay for college. He was a quick study and earned his bachelor's degree in civil engineering in less than four years. Bradley worked hard, turning a small engineering firm into a multi-million dollar business.

Twenty years later, Bradley Juniper wanted to make a difference. Delving into politics, he ran against the incumbent in Atlanta's mayoral election. Bradley's kind, matter-of-fact way of dealing with difficult topics boosted his popularity. No one ever expected he would win the majority.

His constituents sensed they could always rely on Mayor Juniper's honesty and commitment. After serving as mayor for four years, he ran for the Governor's seat. Again, his flawless history and charming personality convinced nearly the entire state of Georgia to vote for him.

Six years later, Bradley Juniper became the official Republican Presidential candidate. His campaign promises involved work and education incentives, as well as keeping jobs in America. He believed employers should provide equal pay for equal work.

Governor Juniper responded to a late afternoon phone call from President Langford. "Madam President, did I understand correctly? You are backing out of the election?"

"Yes, that is correct, Bradley. But that wasn't the only reason why I called you. You see, I'd like to support you as the Republican candidate. I've always admired your tenacious spirit and commitment to justice."

Governor Juniper grinned as he wiped the beads of sweat from his brow and leaned back in his chair. "I'm humbly grateful, Madam President, but I am curious. Why me?"

Robin responded, "I prefer someone not caught up in the political madness. Quite frankly, you don't strike me as someone who'd tolerate socialistic views."

"You are correct. I can't bear to watch the government create more giveaway programs that would further suffocate the national debt and cripple the middle class in the process." He'd always been a firm believer in the philosophy of teaching a person to fish. "President Langford, thanks again for your full support."

"Of course, I don't agree with everything on the Republican docket, like fracking." Robin made that point clear.

Bradley responded, "I understand. Look, I'm not a big fan of it myself. I'm just looking to create more jobs. Perhaps there is a less invasive type of fracking that would lessen adverse impacts on the environment."

Robin rolled her eyes. "I don't even think you really believe that. Anyway, we'll just have to agree to disagree when it comes to fracking. Anyhow, I'm going to alert the press tomorrow. I'm sure there will be tons of questions; should be fun."

Nodding his head, he offered his condolences for her husband's sudden passing. "I know this can't be easy on you, but I hope you know if there's anything I can do to lessen your burden, please don't hesitate to call."

"Thanks, Bradley. That means a lot to me."

After the conversation ended, Bradley Juniper turned on the television to check on the latest news updates. He turned up the volume and shook his head when he witnessed the Democratic candidate, Kelly Farrah, condemning coal mining operations. The subtitles indicated she had been standing in front of Little Blue Run Lake on the West Virginia/Pennsylvania border.

Kelly's short blonde hair was being blown by the wind. She stared into the camera lens with big green eyes, like a deer looks into the headlights. She promised to eliminate future environmental catastrophes like this one from reoccurring.

Bradley couldn't believe his ears. He knew the truth about Little Blue Run Lake. The lake was an artificial lake, completed in 1975 to dilute over 20 billion gallons of coal ash. He huffed, "Get your facts straight, Ms. Farrah!"

Chapter 6 – Adam Pratt

The grunt work had been laid out for the day. Wages were lower than expected at a bituminous coal mine just outside of Beckley, West Virginia. Nobody ever dared to complain. They feared the boss, J. D. Mumpett, who bullied anyone who didn't do what was expected.

Holding a clipboard, J. D. shouted orders. "Adam and Abdul, you'll both be on the early shift this quarter. Report here tomorrow morning by 6 a.m. Got it?"

Abdul shouted, "Yes, sir!"

Adam was annoyed with Abdul who was always kissing up to the boss. He just lowered his head, exhausted after finishing a long twelve hour shift.

Adam Pratt understood decent jobs were hard to come by in this area. He dropped out of school at the age of 14. Living in a small shack, off the grid, with his father who'd been out of work yet again. This rural town of West Virginia was the only place Adam had really ever known. Scrambling to make enough to purchase meals for one week, he lied about his age so he could work at the coal mine.

*****

"Damn liberals have ruined America!" Adam's father was having another drunken fit over politics. He balked as he read a day-old newspaper that had been found in a trash bin outside of the local market. He preferred to blame his economic situation on President Langford.

Adam glanced at the recycling bin that was filled to the brim with empty beer cans. Then he looked down at his own coal miner's hands. *You'd never admit to your poor choices, Dad.*

Chapter 7 – New Commander in Chief

President Langford welcomed President Juniper and his wife, Rebecca, as they arrived at the White House. She handed Rebecca a lovely bouquet of flowers. Then they made their way to the Oval Office where Robin Langford offered some practical advice.

Robin walked over to a coffee table with two small gifts wrapped in gold. She handed them to President Juniper. The first one contained a 14k gold Presidential pin.

"Thank you! I love it!" He immediately pinned it to his lapel. Then he opened the second box. He held up the mug and read aloud the inscription, "I'm in charge now." He and his wife burst out laughing.

President Juniper enthusiastically reacted, "You're too funny, Robin! I will put it right here on my desk. Good one!"

After a nice long conversation, President Langford said her goodbyes and departed the

White House. As she was escorted to Marine One, a feeling of melancholy overcame her.

*****

The news media was covering the Presidential Inauguration and the parade. They were already speculating about President Juniper's decision not to attend any Presidential balls. Many assumed it was because of what happened to President Langford.

No one understood that he wanted to get a head start on his duties as the new head of the Executive Branch.

*****

President Juniper was perched behind the nineteenth-century Resolute desk in the Oval Office. He looked over at the Chief of Staff. "Frank, it's been about one week since my transition to Commander in Chief. First thing's first, we'll need to address how to support businesses and encourage people to get back to work."

Frank Wilson was a stout, wily fellow with sagging cheeks. Previous experience working with members of Congress prepared him for navigating the political arena. "Mr. President, we'll need to prove your proposed plan will work in order to gain approval from both parties."

President Juniper paused to consider the options. "Perhaps…" He shifted his weight in his executive chair, leaning back. With his right elbow pressed into the armrest, he cradled his chiseled jaw with his hand. "I'm not that sure Congress would want to overturn crippling decisions of handing out money for doing nothing. Businesses are permanently shutting down because they cannot find help. Americans need better work incentives."

Frank advised, "Past administrations have raised the minimum wage threshold, but history has shown this has made inflation worse! The status of our economy hovers in a delicate balance."

The President nodded in agreement. "Let's reexamine the unemployment benefits that were modified under Gerry Langford."

*****

Christine Welch, President Juniper's Secretary of Defense, entered the room. "Mr. President, you must see this." She grabbed the television remote and switched it on. It was showing live news updates at the US/Mexican border. "We believe there are valid reasons for concern. Criminals and potential terrorists could be streaming in without the proper background checks. Sir, we strongly believe this is a national security risk."

President Juniper intended to keep another campaign promise, increasing security in America. He ordered two thousand troops to the southern border crossings in Texas and California to prevent unauthorized entry.

Christine briefed President Juniper about two more possible threats from established terrorist organizations in Iran and Afghanistan.

President Juniper needed to take all threats seriously. He understood there were legitimate hardships and each situation needed to be evaluated. His hazel eyes revealed his emotions when he watched the horrifying video clips of children being dropped over the border wall by smugglers wearing face masks to hide their identities. "Jeez, I cannot believe it! Where are the parents? And why aren't they being charged with child neglect?"

The President firmly placed both hands on his desk and stood up. "We have laws in this country. If a single parent in this country leaves a small child home alone to provide for the family, that poor parent gets penalized. Tell me, how is this situation any different?"

Press Secretary, Harold Kowolsky, nervously combed through his thinning salt and pepper hair with trembling fingers. "Sir, what would you like me to convey to the media this afternoon?"

President Juniper was now positioned in front of his desk. He abruptly loosened a navy striped tie around his rugged neck and leaned back against the front edge of the mahogany stained desk. Facial moisture caused his dark rimmed glasses to slide forward. He pushed the specs back into place, contemplating his options. "Harold, I trust you will tell them the truth. That we will need to assess the situation in person. It's a terrible scenario and I realize there are legitimate hardships, but there is no telling who has already entered our country. To put it mildly, that scares the hell out of me! A crowd of radical terrorists could be crossing as we speak, seeking asylum in the good ole USA. I don't understand how this could have been overlooked."

"Sir, what should we do about the media coverage at the border?" The Press Secretary had been trying to stifle the negative publicity.

President Juniper nodded his head in acknowledgement. "Freedom of the press, I suppose. Let's see if we can set up some kind of transitioning system so everybody is properly documented. I want there to be legal representation for those who have a valid reason to be here. It is critical that we ensure the southern border is properly secured."

Mario Caesar, the Secretary of Homeland Security, spoke up. "Sir, last night we uncovered a tunnel under an old section of the border wall. It appears drug lords have been illegally smuggling illegal contraband into the US. Thanks to a local farmer in the region who reported suspicious activity, our military is in the process of destroying it as we speak."

"Good,… uh, Harold make a note of that so we can share that with reporters."

President Juniper worked with his advisors to create an emergency program using the acronym, SSSN (Safe Social Sponsoring Network). Designed to grant 10,000 people per year temporary work visas to live and work within the United States until a court date could be set to review the hardships.

The President was adamant. "We must step up national security measures in order to prevent future terrorism on American soil. Maybe we could extend incentive rewards to those who abide by our laws."

President Juniper called up one of his aides. "Brenda, would you please arrange transportation to the southern border?" She worked alongside the Secret Service to coordinate travel plans for the President and his Cabinet.

After the staff meeting ended, the television remained on. President Juniper cringed when he overheard annoying remarks from the Democratic Party, accusing him of being a racist.

President Juniper recognized it was a political weapon used to turn public opinion against him. But he felt hurt and offended. He resented this ploy and needed to clear the air. "Polly, I'd like to set up a meeting with Leonard Higgins, President of the NAACP."

"Yes, Sir, Mr. President…" Polly Arnold was the only Democrat on President Juniper's team. When the news media got wind of that, they tried to make a big deal out of it. She quickly and professionally shot down their negative commentary when she spoke in full support and admiration of her boss.

As a proud American with North African roots, President Juniper jumped many hurdles in his life. With the Democrats trying to make him look bad, he refused to let false accusations run amuck.

Chapter 8 – Reunion

Secret Service Agent Steve Flex received a phone call from a dear friend. "Well, if it isn't Special Agent Vern! Long time, no see! How are you?"

"Still fighting bad guys. And you?" Ann smirked as she remembered the last case they worked on together.

"Never better. So what do I owe this pleasure?" Steve had been keeping busy with security details for President Langford and her family. Ann often crossed his mind. She was not easy to forget.

"I've been working on this case for a while. I might need another set of eyes. Would you be interested?"

"Well, I don't see why not." Steve was flattered she wanted his assistance.

"Let's meet up for dinner at our favorite haunt. How does 7 o'clock sound?"

"Perfect, looking forward to it." After the conversation, Steve ruminated over one obvious fact. *She needs my help.*

*****

Maxi's Diner was nearly empty when Ann arrived. She noticed an elderly couple sitting next to a glass cylinder with a tempting array of revolving desserts. Privacy was a priority; there was too much at stake. Ann couldn't risk being overheard. She moved to a booth at the opposite corner, took off her overcoat and positioned herself so she could see the front door.

The waitress handed her a menu.

"Could I please have another menu? I'm meeting a friend."

"Sure thing, can I get you anything to drink while you wait?"

"Tea would be lovely. Thank you."

*****

Ann's heartbeat sped up when Steve walked into the place ten minutes later. A captivating smile told her that he was happy to see her. Wearing tight fitting jeans, it was obvious Steve kept himself in tip top condition. His black leather jacket glistened in the light, revealing a snug teal polo. A dark brown faux-hawk hairstyle practically matched his dark brown eyes.

Ann inhaled and straightened her posture. Natural long wavy red hair complimented her dazzling green eyes. Sipping on tea, her cranberry lips left a curved stain on the edge of the ceramic cup.

They locked eyes, as he casually walked over. "I see you've reserved the perfect spot." He slid into the booth next to her, rather than across. It was the logical choice, considering they both liked keeping an eye on who was coming and going. He leaned in and delivered a friendly peck on the cheek.

"Thanks for meeting me here. I'm at a standstill with a group of murder cases that could be related. Perhaps you might see something I've missed. The suspects we've interviewed so far seem to have an alibi. Steve, it's completely mind boggling!" Ann was one of the few people in Steve Flex's life who actually called him by his first name. Everybody else referred to him as Flex.

Ann's eyebrows lifted with emotion as her lips completed a seductive pout. Her soft glowing complexion mesmerized him.

Steve casually ran his hand along the back of his neck. "I'd be happy to look it over with you. Would you like to get started on it tonight?"

Ann nodded, "The sooner the better… Quite frankly, it's been keeping me awake at night. I've been running into dead ends. My partner, Karen, who I also consider to be a good friend, suggested I reach out to other agencies when she received a call to help the CIA in Texas. You were at the top of that list, since you have more than adequate skills and a high clearance level."

Agent Flex was a Navy Seal before becoming an integral part of the Secret Service.

Flattered that Agent Vern remembered him after all this time, he grinned at the notion of teaming up once again.

*****

After dinner, Steve went back to Ann's place. Her spare bedroom was large enough to accommodate a home office. Neatly stacked manilla files were on the corner of a hardwood cherry-stained desk. Looking at the pile more closely, he noticed they were arranged in chronological order. Impeccable organization skills were one of the many traits he admired about her.

Ann grabbed a thinner folder from the top of the pile and pulled out a group of paper clipped items. The first page contained a summary of events. Underneath, verbatim transcripts of possible witnesses who'd been hiking in the area. "Twenty-two dead bodies have been found on or near the Appalachian Trail. All of them appear to have been murdered. The most recent dead body was discovered two weeks ago."

Steve asked, "Hmm, I wonder what these victims had in common?"

"We're still trying to figure that out." Ann slid off her high-heeled pumps and wandered into the walk-in closet. As she was changing into more comfortable clothes, she shared some more observations. "Autopsy results reveal different causes of death. There was a stabbing, a strangulation, a poisoning, and a drowning. The drowning victim had been a champion swimmer in high school. Figuring out how these people are linked will help us pinpoint who might have wanted them dead."

Steve felt warm, he took off his jacket and slung it over a desk chair before he sat down. Humbly oblivious about how his shirt accentuated his chiseled muscles, he clicked the switch on a nearby desk lamp and opened the first victim's file. His concentration was almost unbreakable until Ann came out in a white cotton t-shirt.

"Would you like some tea or coffee?"

"Tea sounds good." Steve dismissed his x-rated thoughts and returned his focus on the contents in the file.

Picking up his mobile phone, Steve compared news-worthy events with the locations, dates, and times of death. He didn't see anything odd that stood out. Determined to find a connection, he foraged through more files. *Wonder if any were registered at...? Hmm...*

His curiosity led him to consider the *Trail Journals* website. Agent Flex had his own account on that site. He tried to access journals that might include posts with photographs of the victims. In deep concentration, he was startled when Ann returned with two steaming cups.

"Here you go. Careful, it's hot."

He politely thanked her and carefully set it down on a nearby coaster. He pointed to some recent blogs on *Trail Journals*. "I was just checking out this *Trail Journals* website."

Ann peered over his shoulder. "Hmm, interesting… I'm not familiar with that one."

"Yeah, its for hikers along the Appalachian Trail so they can post updates about their progress. Family and friends use it to keep up with their loved ones. But some blogs contain photographs and I was thinking we might be able to match some of the victims' photos."

Ann leaned in closer, "We'll have to try and figure out their real names. Look, all of them are using nicknames."

Steve explained, "That's because everyone is encouraged to use fictitious names for safety reasons. Perhaps, the ranger keeps both legal and trail names in a database. That could save us a bunch of time." He also knew not everybody liked to post photos of themselves on the internet.

Ann contemplated it for a moment. "I'd already checked all of the standard social media websites, but nothing stood out as odd. How did you find out about this one?"

"Right after I came back from Afghanistan, I needed to clear my head. I decided to hike the Appalachian Trail from Springer Mountain to Katahdin, Maine. My trail name was *Iron Jack*."

"Wow! That was some feat! How long did it take you to complete?"

"Oh, about five months… Here, I'll pull up my blog so you can get an idea." As he scrolled through the photographs and posts, he glanced over at Ann who had been staring in awe.

"I'm impressed, Iron Jack!"

Steve was a modest man, he smiled and returned his gaze to the phone.

He showed her what he discovered thus far. "Let's look at the first victim." He scrolled down through the posts with images. "Here we go!" He found a blog feed with photos that closely resembled a victim. "Looks like Arthur Brown used the name *Brown Bear*."

"I knew you'd find something we might be able to use. Hey, if you ever want a career working for the FBI, I can put in a good word for you." Ann seriously meant it.

Ann's flattery made him blush again. Steve watched her reposition another chair next to him. He got a brief glimpse of what was under her t-shirt and tried to look the other way.

Clearing his throat, he downplayed her compliment. "Awe, you would have discovered it soon enough. I'm sure of it."

Another hour went by, they were sifting through more blogs, comparing photos. After gulping the rest of his tea, he swiveled in the chair and they inadvertently bumped knees. Blushing, he responded, "Oops. My apologies…"

For several seconds, Steve found himself getting lost in her eyes. There was a magnetic pull he could not deny. She must have felt it too because she leaned toward him, gently pressing her forehead against his.

Unable to fight his desires any longer. He initiated a simple kiss, feeling her supple lips against his. His eyes widened in fear when he suddenly realized what he'd just done. He cleared his throat and glanced at the computer screen, clueless about what to say next.

Ann reacted by gently placing a hand on his shoulder. He turned back again to look into her eyes, but hesitated. This time she initiated the kiss, but it was much more passionate. Ann's head arched back as he planted tender kisses down her slender neck. He stroked her beautiful hair.

Steve's hands found hers and he gripped them. "Ann, maybe we…" But before he could even finish the sentence, she kissed him again. His head was swimming and then she manipulated his shirt up and over his head. Kissing his bare chest, she reached down and unbuttoned his jeans.

Steve scooped her up into his arms and set her down on the bed. He stepped out of his jeans and kneeled over her, pausing briefly to take in her beauty. Ann reached around the back of his neck and pulled him in toward her, wrapping her slender legs around his lower back.

He couldn't remember the last time he felt like this about anyone. Steve's dedication to the job made it impossible to date.

*****

"Steve, that was amazing!"

He cradled her in his arms. He blushed again. "Yes, it certainly was." Keeping conversation to a minimum, he was afraid of falling too hard or saying the wrong thing. The last thing he wanted was to screw up a friendship.

Ann grinned. "I must confess, I've had a school girl crush on you ever since we first met."

Steve's voice went up an octave. "Really? I suppose I have a confession to make too. I've been wanting to call you ever since we last parted ways, but I was afraid of scaring you off." After he opened his heart, he hoped he hadn't revealed too much.

Chapter 9 – Springtime Plans

Melody and Peggy met with Deputy Director Phloeb who just finished mulling over all of the security details concerning their hiking trip. "I've assigned Agents Bixben and Flex to be your personal body guards. And I'll be contacting the ranger in Harpers Ferry to register your names. So I'll need to know your trail names, ASAP."

Phloeb felt it was critical that the girls keep a low profile. Their safety depended on it. The girls were entitled to a little rest and relaxation without the tabloids making a big fuss over it.

Peggy crossed her arms in front. "Do we really need to have two agents looking after us? I was sort of hoping we'd be able to finally cut back on the whole security entourage thing. Since our mother is no longer active President, would you consider just one agent instead of two?"

He clenched his jaw before letting out a sigh. "You're correct about having that option, however, I would advise against it, especially since dead bodies have turned up near that part of the trail." He hoped this would change her mind even though she was correct about waving mandatory security measures.

Melody batted her eyelashes and folded her hands, "I'm okay with that too. Maybe you could let us have Agent Bixben?"

Director Phloeb paused to think about it. He paced back and forth before responding. "All right, I'll notify Bixben." Phloeb figured with Carter Bixben's Navy Seal background, the girls would be in good hands.

"Bixben, change of plans. You're going solo with the Langford sisters' in mid March."

Agent Bixben responded, "Aye-aye… Sure thing, sir!"

Phloeb's stone cold expression hid the fact that he was concerned. Deep down, he hoped one agent would be sufficient should anything happen. *Bixben is one of my best agents. Perhaps I'm overthinking it.*

Peggy jotted down their trail names and handed it to Phloeb. Peggy chose *Sisterwood* since this was a sisterly bonding trip in the woods. Melody chose *Opal Bound,* which was fitting because Opal was the name given to her by the Secret Service under her mother's Presidency.

Phloeb shook his head and smiled. "Alrighty then, Bixben will be arriving here shortly."

*****

Bixben needed to be involved with the hiking plans even though Peggy laid out every detail. He never minded her bossiness, as long as it didn't interfere with their safety.

The girls were competitive and wanted to hike in four states, totaling 43.5 miles. They would start at the Virginia/West Virginia border and hike through Maryland, crossing into Pennsylvania. They'd been preparing an escape from reality for a while.

*****

As youngsters, Peggy and Melody loved camping and hiking with their parents. Classified as tomboys in school, they shared a love for nature and a quest for adventure. Fond memories of the family ranch would often come up whenever they reminisced about the old days.

After Peggy's seven-year marriage failed, she took an accounting position at Lockheed Martin. Soon after the assassination attempt on her mother's life, she decided it was best to return to the East coast. Working as a government-appointed accountant for almost three years, Peggy was looking forward to getting away with her sister. With three unused weeks on the books, she'd been past due for a proper vacation. Disconnecting from city life for a little while would be a welcome change.

Unlike Peggy, marriage was never an option for Melody. Her work schedule made it impossible for a love life. The closest she came to walking down the aisle was when she had been engaged to Grant Pearl in her Freshman year of college. He seemed like the perfect guy, until she learned he was hiding a secret. When she discovered he had a boyfriend on the side, her heart was shattered. She pulled back, relinquishing any thoughts of a long-term relationship.

As Peggy's younger sister, Melody worked at Prospective Engineering, Inc. in Maryland. It was a large geological engineering firm with satellite offices in 20 different States. With her credentials, she could go anywhere, but chose to stay close to her mother.

The EPA in Pennsylvania and West Virginia received a surge of complaints from residents and businesses near fracking industries. Melody's firm in Washington DC was hired to work with various agencies to test the soil for ground pollutants.

Morton Hendrix, the CEO of Merifrack, sharply accused Melody of being biased against fracking, based on her association with President Langford. Pending lawsuits against many fracking corporations forced them to hire additional expert witnesses.

"Ground samples don't lie." Melody would often repeat those words whenever she was confronted. She was always careful to send out an independent crew to gather the evidence. It was crucial to keep the testing process transparent by individually labeling the samples with barcodes. That was done so no one in the lab would know where the material had been collected. This ensured quality control.

*****

"Melody, did you pack your backpack yet? Three days until we leave all the stress behind us." Peggy's voice contained a hint of anxious anticipation.

Melody was more laid back than Peggy. "I'll take care of it tomorrow." She noticed her sister's backpack already propped up against the back corner near the doorway. It was bulging at the seams. "Peg, you sure ya want to pack all of that?" Melody made a valid point.

Chapter 10 – The Envelope

Early Saturday morning, after making love, Brent Volt's long time girlfriend, Amanda Sky, brought up the topic of marriage. "Let's run off to Vegas and get married!"

Brent yawned and rolled out of bed. Then he wrapped a blue terrycloth robe around himself and wandered into the bathroom, "Look, you know I love you, babe. Marriage has always been a sore spot for me. Why muck up a good thing?" He was referring to his first two marriages that failed.

Before they could debate the topic any further, the door closed and the shower was running.

*****

With a wrapped towel around his slender waist, Brent exited the bathroom. "How about we go have a nice breakfast at that little bakery that just opened last week?"

There was no reply. Brent balanced on one leg to step into his khaki Dockers. He glanced around the dimly lit bedroom, wondering if Amanda might have drifted off to sleep.

A narrow beam of light was coming from a partially open doorway leading into the hallway. "Babe?"

Not bothering to put on a shirt, he opened the door and fled downstairs.   It wasn't like Amanda to get out of bed this early on a Saturday morning. "Amanda?"

He rounded the corner and moved toward the kitchen.

Click!

Brent suddenly felt the cold nozzle of a pistol pressed up against the base of his skull. He immediately lifted his hands in the air. "Just,… just take the wallet out of my left pocket, okay?"

A raspy male voice with a thick accent responded. "That's not what I want! Sit down!" He placed his large hand on Brent's left shoulder and shoved him down into a chair.

The intruder shined the flashlight on Amanda, who was gagged and tied to another chair.

Brent hollered, "What do you want from us?"

"Your cooperation... I have an urgent message for your boss." Then he handed Brent a sealed legal-sized envelope. "It's critical that you deliver this. Don't let anyone else open it! Keep the authorities out of it or you'll regret it. I've been keeping an eye on you both, so if you're smart, you'll do exactly what you're told. You don't want me to come back, it won't be pretty."

"Wait… What's this all about?" Brent heard the front door shut and turned his head in response. The mysterious man vanished.

Running over to a nearby window, Brent shifted the curtain over just enough to get a good look at a tall figure wearing a ski mask, scooting across the street. The man ducked into a compact car with dark tinted windows and sped off.

Visibly shaken, Brent was rapidly breathing, trying to process the horrifying encounter. Still clutching the padded envelope in his clammy hand, he spun around when he heard a muffled voice.

It was Amanda. "Mmm! Mmmm!"

Brent snapped out of his daze. "Shit!" He rushed over to Amanda's side and removed the duct tape with his free hand. Then he momentarily set the envelope down so he could untie her.

Amanda threw her arms around Brent, tears streamed down her cheeks. Then she pulled back trying to catch her breath, "Brent, Whaa… What just happened here?"

"I don't know, babe. But I have a strong feeling these people have been watching us for a while. Last week, when I left the coffee shop on the way to work, I could have sworn I was being followed, but dismissed it."

She placed her fingers at her temples. "Dang! Remember when I received that mysterious bouquet of flowers at the office last Wednesday? I thought they were from you. The card was blank inside."

Brent vaguely remembered she'd spoken about it. "Did you ever find out who actually sent them? I just assumed it was from one of your clients." He knew she was a successful real estate agent and occasionally received thank you gifts.

She shook her head in reply. "I thought so too, but decided to find out just so I'd know who to thank. When I contacted the florist, they told me it was paid for in cash and sent from a gentleman named Oscar Gordon. He used the address of a nearby pharmacy and nobody's ever heard of him."

"That is odd. Amanda, why didn't you tell me about that?"

"I really didn't think much about it. I was too busy showing houses."

He looked down at the envelope again. "I can tell you one thing. I have no idea what this is all about and I'm not sure I want to know either."

*****

Monday morning, at the Pentagon, Brent arrived twenty minutes before his shift had been scheduled to begin. The instructions the gunman gave were to give the envelope to his boss. He worked closely with high ranking generals and other prominent members of the Department of Defense. But his boss was Christine Welch, the Secretary of Defense.

Brent's nerves had been on edge since Saturday's encounter. As he approached his work station, he saw Christine standing in the corridor engaged in conversation with General George Whitlock. *I need to speak with her. At the very least, she needs to know what happened.*

Placing his coat in his chair, he laid the envelope on top. Keeping up with his normal routine, he popped a coffee pod in the machine and filled it with water. Then he stuck his head out of his office just in time to see General Whitlock walk by.

The General greeted Brent in a baritone voice. "Good morning!"

Brent properly saluted the General and responded, "Good morning, sir." Then he walked toward Christine Welch's office.

Knocking on the door jamb, "Do you have a minute? Something's come up that requires your immediate attention."

"Please, come in. What is it, Brent?" Christine couldn't help but notice his pasty pallor.

"I thought you should know that my girlfriend and I were held at gunpoint Saturday morning. Threats were made if I didn't fully cooperate. I was handed this envelope and told to deliver it to you."

"What? That's awful! Did you contact the authorities?"

Brent sighed, "That wasn't an option. I suspect this person's been watching our every move. I didn't know what else to do."

Christine calmly derived a plan of action. "I suppose if it were any type of explosive device, security would have discovered it when you entered the building. Follow me. We'll take extra precautions and get straight to the bottom of it." She unlocked a large subsidiary supply closet filled with war time necessities and retrieved protective gear.

Christine shoved the items into a large canvas bag. "We don't want to draw attention. Just accompany me to the central courtyard."

*****

The wind was quelled by five surrounding walls. It was a bright and sunny day with a hint of crisp cool air.

Christine maintained her composure. "Brent, here, take my phone. I need you to record me opening the package. If there should be any issues, we shall document it all."

Before recording, they both donned the safety gear. Brent chuckled at the absurdity. "Just an ordinary day at the Pentagon…"

Christine had been out of ear shot. "Okay, Brent, ready to start recording?"

"Yes, ma'am!" He introduced the evidence while embedding the date and time in the video sequence.

"This is Christine Welch. I've been delivered an anonymous package at the Pentagon through Brent Volt, who was held against his will at gunpoint on Saturday morning. Though I am side stepping security protocols, I believe it will protect Brent and his family from threats that were made. As you can see, we have taken extra safety measures. Okay, here it goes…"

Tearing off a corner, she ran a latex covered index finger along the top seam and split open the envelope. Pinching the clipped bundle of papers inside, she carefully lifted them out. No foreign matter had been visible. Through the steamy mask, she read the cover letter.

Brent watched helplessly as Christine's demeanor change from lighthearted curiosity to sheer terror. Continuing to film the entire event, he was cautious not to ask.

After Christine turned the page, Brent witnessed her collapse to the ground in a kneeling position.

"Christine! Christine!" He dropped the phone and rushed over to her. Brent could only briefly see that it was a photograph.

Christine's sobbing was muffled in the mask. She was clearly affected by the contents of this package. Brent wasn't good at comforting others. He did his best to soothe his boss. "What can I do to help? Please tell me how I can help!"

She could barely get the words out, "Terrorists… h-holding m-my family hostage."

"What? Shit! I'm so sorry! Christine, I had no idea." Brent couldn't believe what was happening.

Brent helped her back up, though she still appeared unsteady. "Christine, I'll contact General Whitlock! Don't worry, we'll come up with a rescue plan." He picked up the packet with gloved hands and inserted it into a clear plastic bag. Then he retrieved her phone and escorted her back to the office.

*****

The details needed to be revealed to the Department of Defense's top security officers and Mario Caesar, Secretary of Homeland Security. If this was a terrorist event, Mario needed to know about it.

According to the stipulations in the letter, the United States' military had been requested to stand down at the southern border, looking the other way so foreigners could cross the US border without deterrence.

This would go against President Juniper's policies. He'd entrusted Christine and Mario with the border issues. She was being forced to go behind the Commander in Chief's back to comply with the terrorist's demands in order to save her family.

Chapter 11 - Trail Journals

A large group of hikers gathered in a bunkhouse. Details of the previous evening's deadly discovery came up in conversation. Rumors and speculation about a possible serial killer were being passed along the Appalachian Trail's hiker network.

Many hikers decided to hang up their boots and go home. Others pressed on, despite the terrifying stories. They'd trained too hard to quit now. Believing there was some truth to the saying, *safety in numbers*, they formed multiple walking groups.

Seventy-year old Samuel Regis was one of the hikers who decided to continue. He had gained quite a following on the *Trail Journals* website, blogging under the nickname, *Bootlegger9*. Embellishing facts about the tragic deaths, he craved attention, never missing an opportunity to shed more light on himself. People who knew Samuel well, would label him as a chronic complainer and a drama king.

His blogs were being followed by more than 400 people. Samuel couldn't let his virtual audience down. He felt it was his duty to keep everyone informed, despite the inaccuracy and misinformation.

Samuel had been paired up with a group who just barely tolerated him. They purposely withheld personal stories to avoid becoming headline news online. They wanted no part of his negatively tinged rhetoric.

Chapter 12 – Harpers Ferry

Hikers on the Appalachian Trail in West Virginia were jolted awake as tectonic plates shifted below. Tents mischievously swayed in a campground near Harpers Ferry.

Mr. and Mrs. Ferndale, a retired married couple, instantly woke up and held onto each other inside the tent, not understanding what was happening. In the next few seconds, they heard car alarms going off in the distance.

*****

Anyone who read Samuel Regis's hiking posts had been aware of his tendencies to complain about everything. He even blamed a hiking boot company for failing to create a boot that was stable enough to withstand earthquakes. He exaggerated about how he almost fell off a cliff and died.

Samuel was oblivious to his own negative, draining personality. The hiking group left him behind, walking at a much faster pace to avoid engaging in chat.

*****

Approximately one hundred miles north of Harpers Ferry, another pair of early morning hikers had become unsteady on their feet when the earth trembled. Among a field of jagged boulders, Mark Spieler and Norman Conrad crouched down low, like pouncing tigers. They reached out instinctually gripping the sharp granite. With jaws clenched, Mark Spieler and Norman Conrad waited several minutes for the seismic activity to cease.

Norman shouted, "Whoa! What the hell was that?"

Mark replied, "Jeez, felt like an earthquake or something."

Norman scrunched up his face, "In these parts… ? Nah, that ain't right. Betcha it was an explosion somewhere." Norman liked to think he knew what he was talking about. He never finished high school, opting to become a full time laborer in a small West Virginia suburb.

Mark wasn't buying Norman's theory. "What makes you so sure?"

Norman elaborated, "Well, fracking makes everything unstable. I should know, I seen what they did at my uncle's fracking business. Ya ain't gonna tell me all that damn drillin' ain't causin' some kind of ruckus!"

Mark shrugged his shoulders, dismissing Norman's reply. He was busy trying to surf for a better explanation on his phone, but there wasn't any cell service. "Dang it!"

Although east coast earthquakes were less prominent than west coast quakes, vibrations along eastern tectonic plates traveled farther than those on the western coast of the US. Many residents in the area attributed the earth shaking event to the fracking that was encroaching into the main fault line.

Mark and Norman decided to take a break. They'd already hiked more than four miles that morning.

When cell service returned, Mark jumped onto the *Trail Journals* website and logged in, curious to see if anyone posted about the quake.

Mark snickered, "Hey, Norman! Get a load of this! What an asshole! This guy wants to blame the company who made his shoes because they didn't hold him up when the ground was shaking."

Norman summed it up, "Sounds like a damn Yankee-doodle pansy!"

*****

Twenty minutes later, the USGS (United States Geological Survey) issued an initial estimated report regarding that morning's earthquake. The magnitude had been measured at 5.3 and was centered 10 miles north of Harpers Ferry.

Mark studied the map. "Maybe we can camp here tonight. It's about three miles out."

"Sure thing…"

Before Mark and Norman resumed the northbound trek, they rehydrated and repositioned their backpacks. Carefully maneuvering around the rocks slowed down progress.

Norman realized his left shoe was untied. He stopped. "Dang it!"

Mark turned around. "What?"

"Ah, nothin' … got some loose shoestrings. Go ahead. I'll catch up." Norman sat down on a large tree trunk that had rotted out at the bottom and collapsed.

Norman bent over and tightly double knotted it. He thought he saw something out of the corner of his eye. Whipping his head around, he saw an empty bag of Quicklime that was partially buried. *People are slobs!* Then he wondered why it was there. It wasn't like a person would be doing gardening out here.

Norman got up and looked around. The hair on his back stood up on end when he saw a small piece of curly brown hair flapping in the wind. The hair did not look like it belonged to an animal. He hoped maybe someone was just taking a snooze behind the giant boulder in the shade, but his gut instinct was nagging at him. *What if someone needs help?*

He always hated these types of scenes in horror films, yet here he was out in the middle of nowhere on the Appalachian Trail. *Shit!* He didn't realize he was holding his breath. Cautiously approaching the large moss covered rock, he paused for a moment to gather enough courage to look. *I'm a damn chicken shit!*

It was the adrenaline that kicked in and made him step beyond the massive granite piece. But his stomach curdled when he looked down and saw a grayish-white corpse with multiple stab wounds covered in a white substance. "Ahhhh!"

Mark heard Norman's screams and turned around immediately. Mark did not have to backtrack too far.

He found Norman sitting on the same tree trunk where he'd tied his shoes. Mark could see him holding his stomach and rocking. It looked like he'd seen a ghost. "Norman! What the hell happened? Did you see a bear or something?"

Norman could only shake his head and say, "Dead body… dead body!"

Mark used his cell phone to contact the authorities immediately. He stayed with his friend until the state police arrived.

Later they would learn that the Quicklime had been used to hide the rotting odor from the corpse's putrefaction. The state police decided it was best to notify the FBI concerning the death of Catie Minnow. They feared it might be connected to a series of deaths along the Appalachian Trail.

Chapter 13 - Message

Omar first met Bill Archer at the *Chug it Down Bar and Grille*, a local bar in Williamsport, Pennsylvania, when he was searching for employment. They struck up a conversation and learned they shared common values, especially concerning the environment. In fact, it was Bill that suggested Omar work at Merifrack, Inc.

Omar was puzzled, "Help me understand… You hate fracking. Why would I want to work for a company like that?"

Bill Archer was a retired attorney from Virginia who moved to Williamsport, Pennsylvania. He maintained his membership with the Roanoke Appalachian Trail Club. Spending most of his days fighting for clean water rights, he thought Omar might be able to help. "That's easy, Omar, you could keep an eye on things. If you see any violations, just send me the information with the photos. We'll put everything into a database. Hey, if we play our cards right, we might even be able to shut them down for good."

While Omar contemplated his part in the matter, Bill insisted Omar stay at a rental apartment that he and his wife owned in Williamsport, Pennsylvania. "You'd be doing me a huge favor. All you have to do is report what is happening there. In fact, you don't even have to pay the rent. It's a nice corner unit."

Omar agreed to submit his application to Merifrack. "Sounds easy enough."

*****

Once Omar was hired by Merifrack, Inc. he was extremely disciplined. Early every morning he arrived on the job site before anyone else.

Over the next several months Omar passed along information to Bill concerning hazardous conditions and all breaches in environmental agreements. It was extremely easy to find all of the violations. Occasionally, he would even snap a photo for proof.

Coworkers didn't take well to newcomers who weren't born in America. Their ignorance led to nasty prejudicial remarks directed at

Omar. Mr. Hendrix, Omar's boss, seemed to be the only one who treated Omar with respect.

Omar almost felt bad that he was spying on the boss's business.

Bill Archer was able to collect enough information to have Merifrack shut down a couple of times. Unfortunately, those shut downs never lasted very long. The fracking always resumed.

*****

Bill and his wife of ten years, Connie Archer, never had children. She was in her late fifties when they married. The Archers would often visit Omar. Eventually, they would consider Omar like a son.

Omar kept the apartment neat and tidy. He also agreed to help the Archers whenever they needed repairs done on their vehicles. He liked keeping busy.

The Archers didn't want Omar to take the bus to work anymore. They purchased a used 2015

Honda Fit. It was a standard stick shift and Bill spent three weeks teaching Omar how to drive. Omar's temporary visa allowed him to obtain a driver's license.

*****

One morning, Omar woke up earlier than usual and wandered into the shower. His work attire was already laid out. It was pitch dark outside; the sun wasn't due to rise for another hour.

He checked the weather forecast on his mobile phone, peering at any unread messages. Then he peeled a banana and quickly devoured it. He slid on a lightweight jacket and poured a thermos full of hot coffee and secured the lid. Tucking the vessel into his backpack, he yanked on the refrigerator's handle and grabbed the paper bag with a bologna sandwich and apple inside and added it to the backpack. *There, that should do it.*

The car started on the second try. He put it into gear and drove up the spiraling dirt roadway to the employee parking area near

Well Number 2. The sky was glowing in rich hues of orange and red.

He shut the car door leaving his backpack behind. Then he slid his keys into his right front jeans pocket. Walking the rest of the way up to where he would begin working, he inhaled the cool crisp air.

The sky was becoming brighter with each passing minute. Omar could begin to see shadowy outlines of the drilling machines. One of his daily rituals he liked to do before starting his job was to clean up the site. He retrieved a contractor trash bag from one of the work trucks and filled it with used soda cans and construction debris left behind from the previous work day.

As he approached the dumpster behind one of the rigs, he accidentally tripped on something blocking the way. *What was that?*

When the sun finally peaked through low wispy clouds, casting more light onto the trip hazard, Omar suddenly realized what it was, or rather who it was. The horrific cadaver frightened him, forcing him to flee the scene and drive away.

Omar suspected someone at Merifrack wanted him to find Bill Archer's body. He panicked, fearing he might be next. Perhaps someone figured out what Omar was doing. Either way, the message was clear.

Chapter 14 - Merifrack, Inc.

Morton Hendrix started out as an amateur mechanic at the age of 12 in his father's garage. When he turned 16, he shaved his head bald and joined a Brazilian Jiu Jitsu gym to immerse himself in the world of martial arts. He eventually became a heavyweight UFC fighter. Unfortunately, a severe shoulder injury followed by multiple surgeries forced him to give up that part of his life.

When Morton turned 25 years old, his grandfather passed away and left him an entire hydraulic fracturing business. As the new CEO of Merifrack, Inc. he had much to learn. When his hair failed to grow back, he wore a dark charcoal toupee. It stood out like a sore thumb, but nobody ever mentioned about it. One year after inheriting the business, he married his high school sweetheart.

Morton's pickup truck was maroon in color, though it was camouflaged underneath a heavy layer of dust. He never bothered to wash it, figuring *what's the point?* It wasn't like he could escape daily travel along dirt roads. This was where he spent the majority of his life now. A rear bumper sticker was still visible with Bradley Juniper's campaign slogan in large bold letters, *America First.*

Once the fracking industries resumed operation, Morton hired experienced workers to help him get his grandfather's business up and running again.

Extracting shale gas trapped in coal was not an easy process. He needed to learn all aspects of the fracking operation. Unlike logging where trees could be replaced, fracking left permanent devastation to landscapes and the toxic water runoff polluted nearby lakes and streams. His business was under constant scrutiny thanks to unhappy residents opposed to the operation.

The EPA frequently visited the site, sometimes leaving violation notices and other times completely shutting it down.

Morton's rigs were busy grinding and drilling into the earth. Wells were flooded with a cocktail of industry appropriate chemicals and millions of gallons of water, it was the only viable way to help the shale rock release its natural gas. The machines were expensive to upkeep, but maintenance was crucial because they needed to drill vertically and horizontally for thousands of feet. It was a never-ending process.

Walking over to a picture window in the trailer's office, Morton stood overlooking a containment pond that was being blamed for a myriad of problems. Complaints about the purity of the nearby drinking water sources were a daily annoyance. Morton didn't want to believe there was a problem with toxic wastewater runoff polluting nearby water sheds.

An inspector from the Environmental Protection Agency was due to arrive at Merifrack after 2:00 p.m. Morton needed to be ready for a barrage of questioning that was sure to arise. He couldn't afford to have his entire operation shut down again.

At 11:20 in the morning there'd already been five earthquakes recorded at between 3.0 and

3.6 on the Richter scale. The news reporters loved to throw drilling industries under the bus as a probable cause, despite the presence of fault lines in the area.

With his business still in the red, Morton turned around to pour himself a shot of whiskey. He kept a small flask in his desk for stressful occasions. Although he wasn't considered an alcoholic by his employees, his wife felt he might be headed in a scary direction.

His phone lit up and vibrated. *Jeez, now what?*

Rick, one of Morton's foremen sounded out of breath, "Morty,… better come take a look at this! You're not gonna believe it. We had to stop everything."

He sighed. "Fuck,… now what? Where?"

"We needed to halt operations at the second well."

"Be there in five…Shit!" He disconnected the call and clunked down the full glass of whiskey to rush out to his truck.

Chapter 15 – EPA

Under the Langford Administration, all fracking in the US ceased to exist. But once President Juniper took over, he allowed fracking to resume. He assigned the Environmental Protection Agency with the important task of inspecting and overseeing fracking operations to prevent any environmental catastrophes.

One of the EPA's Region #3 offices was located in Philadelphia, Pennsylvania. They were in charge of issuing fines to any US corporations or individuals that had been violating strict environmental laws.

One specific fracking corporation has received a bunch of violations since it first opened. Merifrack, Inc. was caught spilling toxic fluids into nearby tributaries that drained into Loyalsock Creek. Unfortunately, the consequences never seem to last long. They pay the fines and return to fracking.

The EPA has been unable to pin all of the toxic waste on just one fracking corporation. Unfortunately, each one contributes its own share of problems. Without reinstating another moratorium, the government did little to stop it.

Ulysses Drum worked as an inspector for the EPA. He was constantly receiving calls and complaints involving a 64-mile radius that included the wild mountain region of Pennsylvania and the West Branch of the Susquehanna River. His job was to gather the proof needed to demonstrate how toxic chemicals had been leeching into drinking water sources. After stopping at a local cafe for a cup of coffee, he resumed the route to Upper Fairfield Pennsylvania. He'd met with Morton Hendrix numerous times before, but nothing ever seemed to change. Hendrix just made up excuses or denied that a problem existed.

I've got to piss like a race horse. Cripes! Ulysses turned off the main road in his Ford F250 and meandered along a well-worn dirt road, passing through an open gate with a dangling *No Trespassers* sign. No matter how hard he tried to avoid the ruts, his truck bounced around, making his bladder feel like it might explode.

He stopped the truck and engaged the parking brake. Then he wandered into the woods and carefully looked around before unzipping his trousers and relieving the pressure.

It was unusually quiet and there was no wind. The last time he was up here, there were all sorts of noises from machinery. "Hmm, wonder why it's so quiet? Must be taking a break."

Suddenly, he heard voices tinged with fear and anger. Ulysses couldn't believe what he was overhearing.

"So what're we supposed to do, ignore the fact that there's a dead body out here? Shouldn't we at least call the police or something?"

"Look, I don't have time to deal with this right now. That guy from the EPA will be here any minute. I've gotta go, just hide the body under that blue tarp for now."

Ulysses was startled. *What the hell?* He zipped up his pants and ran back to his truck. Once inside, he rechecked his truck's navigation system. He was only ten minutes away from Hendrix's office.

Moments later, a familiar ringtone was being muffled in his back pocket. Ulysses reached back to retrieve it, engaging the speaker mode so he could talk and drive. He released the emergency brake and peeled out.

His boss, Phil Houlton, director of the EPA, always got straight to the point. "Weren't you planning to meet with Mr. Archer?"

Ulysses answered, "Yeah, after my meeting with Hendrix. Why?"

Phil sighed, "Well, you should know that his wife called. Says he didn't come home last night."

"What? Shit!" Ulysses gulped recalling the conversation he'd just overheard. The thing about that was he hadn't a clue where the chatter was actually coming from. In this area, voices could be carried over long distances. Besides, he was a busy man and a new father. The last thing he needed was to get involved in a complicated investigation.

"You've spoken to Archer more than once, right? Did he ever mention anybody else who might have access to the evidence that Archer wanted to share with us?"

Ulysses was trying to recall a recent conversation. "Yeah, maybe… He mentioned about some guy from Afghanistan helping him. I'm trying to remember, I think the name started with an O…" Fumbling through his mind, he shouted, "Omar! That was it. But I haven't got a clue how to reach him."

"Well, how many people in a small town could possibly be named Omar? Maybe you should hang around there a few more days. After all, we'll pay your expenses."

Ulysses was thinking to himself. *I'll be paying for it in other ways*. He thought about his wife and how stressed she had become with a colicky two month old. But then he thought it might be nice to catch up on some sleep. "I suppose I could stay a little longer."

"That a boy! Fill me in on what you find."

"Will do. Mm'kay, gotta go."

He temporarily pulled over again to place the dreaded call to his wife. He was somewhat relieved when the answer machine picked up. "Hey, babe, uh, Houlton called. He wants me to stay in Williamsport, Pennsylvania to get some things done. I'm sorry. Please call me back when you get this. Love you." *That's going to go over like a fart in church.* He shoved the phone into his back pocket and resumed the journey.

He noticed Hendrix's pickup truck was still making residual ticking noises, an indication that it had been used recently.

The wooden stairs up to the construction trailer creaked under pressure, his cleated work boots retraced the fresh sand laden footprints. Knocking vigorously on the door, he heard a familiar voice.

"Be right there!" Ulysses was convinced it was the same one he'd overheard giving orders to cover the body.

Chapter 16 – "Brown Bear"

"Flex, I don't know if this means anything, but the first Appalachian Trail victim had a PhD in geology and earth science. He's a college professor. He was single; no children."

Agent Flex fumbled with his chin. "There must be a reason why somebody wanted him dead." He said half jokingly, "Maybe he gave one of his students a failing grade…"

Ann grinned. "Anything's possible, I guess. I think we should check out West Virginia University and see what we can learn about Professor Brown."

*****

Agent Flex took a few days off and accompanied Ann to Morgantown, West Virginia.

Arriving late on a Sunday night, they decided to overnight at a nearby B & B. The owner of the establishment smiled. "I'm afraid I only have one room left. There was a college football event this weekend. The room has a lovely view and a king-size bed."

Steve shrugged his shoulders and glanced at Ann for guidance.

Ann casually placed her left hand on his shoulder and answered in a calm tone, "It's fine. We completely understand."

Steve appreciated her taking charge of the awkward situation. He promised himself he would keep things on a professional level. They were here on business after all. He wanted her to know that he respected her. They would need to get some shut eye before tomorrow morning's meeting with the president.

*****

Ann was an early riser, waking up just before 5:00 a.m. She glanced over at Steve and decided she did not want to disturb him. Besides, she hardly ever slept more than five or six hours on any given night. While she took a shower and got dressed, a complimentary newspaper had been slid underneath the door. She combed through her hair, opting to let her hair dry naturally.

Flex tossed and turned most of the night, finally drifting off just before 4:00 a.m. When his phone woke him at 6:30 a.m., he searched blindly for the noise maker, trying to shut it off. After silencing, he squinted at the screen to check for messages. He had one text from Ann that read, "Reading the paper downstairs." *Ugh! It's way too early.* He slowly sat up and pressed both index and middle fingers on his temples.

Taking the stairs down to the breakfast room, he poured himself a fresh cup of coffee and sat down at the same table where Ann had been doing a crossword puzzle in the newspaper.

The owner came over to the table and greeted him. She brought over a small carousel of butter and jam and a basket full of warm croissants. He plucked one from the basket and shoved the flaky delight into his mouth, hoping it would give him the energy he needed to do his job.

Ann looked up from her puzzle and smiled. "I hope you slept well last night."

He sipped his coffee and shrugged one shoulder. He wasn't ready to admit that he couldn't stop thinking about her. Then he lowered the cup. "Well, sort of."

She immediately noticed the dark circles under his eyes. He was much quieter than usual. "Steve, would you rather I drive?"

He covered a yawn with his fist, "That's a wonderful idea; I just need the coffee to kick in."

*****

Pulling into the visitor's parking lot, they walked up to a beautiful brick building and stately clock tower.

Dr. Gregory Terrance, Jr., had been expecting them at 8:00 a.m. After formal introductions, Ann showed him her badge and handed him an official search warrant.

He pulled out two oversized chairs for the pair. "Please sit down. We were saddened to hear about Arthur. He was a valued employee and friend."

Agent Vern asked, "Dr. Terrance, do you have any idea why someone might want to eliminate the professor?"

The president shook his head. "From what I could find out; Professor Brown was well liked by everyone at this university. In fact, he received high ratings on the *Rate My Professor* website."

Agent Flex asked another question, "Do you know if he was involved in any extracurricular activities outside of college?"

"I remember he needed time off. He was being called as an expert witness at a hearing about the new pipeline."

Agent Vern's eyebrows lifted. "When was that?"

Dr. Terrance hesitated for a moment. "Oh, I'm guessing it was over nine months ago."

She quickly scribbled down some notes. "Can you elaborate?"

"I remember him telling me that somebody paid for his expenses."

Flex asked, "Perhaps you could show us the professor's office and classroom?"

"Of course, … follow me."

They watched him pick a key off of one of the hooks by the doorway. Following him down a corridor and through the rear double doors, across the way to another building; they entered the late professor's office which was adjacent to the classroom.

"Dr. Terrance, may we look around?" Agent Flex hoped that his lack of sleep wouldn't cause him to miss important clues.

"Yes, I'll let you do your job. Please, if there's anything else you need, you can find me on my rounds." The president remained in the building and checked on nearby classrooms in session.

Agents Flex and Vern slipped on latex gloves to prevent contaminating evidence.

Ann rummaged through the desk and file cabinets while Flex turned on the laptop computer.

Enter passcode, the computer cursor blinked in a yellow highlighted box. "Shit!" Flex was annoyed with this barricade.

Ann overheard his frustration. She remembered seeing a list of random words in the professor's top desk drawer. "Perhaps it is this last one, since the others are crossed out."

"Only one way to find out…" He carefully typed *Jetlag5* and the screen opened up into a new window. The computer spoke, *"Welcome, Professor. Which app would you like me to open?"*

Unsure if the computer was programmed with voice recognition, he answered, "Recent items".

An hourglass spun around and then a vertical window appeared on the left side of the screen. It showed all recent searches, including the professor's *Trail Journals* blog, a detailed calendar, and midterm grades. One item stood out. It was a document saved in a folder labeled 'pipeline issues' addressed to the county commissioners of five counties (Monroe, Giles, Montgomery, Craig, and Roanoke).

"Ann, this is interesting. The professor wrote a letter to the counties affected by that pipeline. He even copied the Federal Energy Regulatory Commission (FERC). It warned them about catastrophes should there ever be a significant natural disaster, like an earthquake."

"Hmm, let me see that." Ann peered at the screen. "Wow, can you print that out? We might be able to use that."

As the printer whirred, Ann suggested they look at Arthur Brown's personal calendar to find out who he'd recently met with.

She used her phone to take several screen shots of the late professor's digital calendar.

"According to Professor Brown's schedule, he met over six months ago with locals and county commissioners about the pipeline. One month later, he attended another public meeting. There's even a folder that contains the minutes of that meeting. Wow, this guy was extremely organized!"

Ann thought that a printout of the public meeting minutes might provide some insight. Once the printer finished all tasks, she flipped through, speed reading portions of the minutes. "Well, it looks like multiple agencies were in attendance, including the pipeline people." Other companies represented in the minutes were the Interstate Natural Gas Association of America (INGAA) and the US DOT Pipeline and Hazardous Material Safety Administration (PHMSA).

Flex looked at Ann. "Now that I think of it, I remember hearing about that pipeline on the National news a while ago, but then it was never mentioned again."

Ann thought out loud, "Hmm, maybe someone wanted it to just fade away. I can't imagine Valley Wing Pipeline was very happy with the professor. From what I can tell, the professor was adamant about stopping the pipeline project from going through a dangerous geological seismic zone."

Ann went through the last drawer of the file cabinet. She pulled out a bulky folder labeled, *Pipeline Info*. Opening it, she noticed a letter on top addressed to the professor from Bill Archer. "The contents are in chronological order. Hmm, the professor's involvement with the pipeline started approximately one year ago. Bill Archer reached out to Professor Brown. Archer is a member of the Roanoke Appalachian Trail Club. Apparently, there were concerns about the pipeline crossing the Appalachian Trail at Peters Mountain. "

Steve looked up. "I believe that's where a major fault line crosses… May I see those minutes please?" Flex flipped through the pages, pausing to read the part where the professor talks about the risk factors. "Wow, this is fucking batshit!"

Ann observed, "Well, it looks like we've stumbled upon some interesting evidence. I'm going to bag it up."

"I'll let you do your thing. I'm just going to head back into the professor's classroom in case we missed anything. I'll meet you out in the hallway. Dr. Terrance should be around here somewhere." Flex wandered into the cold empty room and looked through the professor's bookshelves and grade books. Nothing seemed odd or out of place, just the usual teaching tools. He exited the classroom and wandered around the empty hallways searching for the president.

A deep voice startled Flex. "How is the search going?" He immediately turned around. It was Dr. Terrance.

"Good, Yes, uh, we won't be able to discuss what we've uncovered, as it goes against investigation protocols. We appreciate your assistance."

"No problem, glad to help. Speaking on behalf of the university, we hope you find out who is behind the professor's tragic death."

Flex shook the president's hand. "Thank you, sir."

Ann caught up with them. She was carrying large waterproof FBI evidence bags containing the professor's laptop and a file folder. "Thanks for your help, Dr. Terrance."

Dr. Terrance issued a polite nod. "Yes, ma'am,… Glad to help."

Chapter 17 – Seismic Zone

The government agencies eventually approved the pipeline project, despite previous opposition. Construction was running ahead of schedule, with less than a week to go. The final details were being put into place. Everything had been going along as planned for Valley Wing Pipeline (VWP).

Martin Drawbuck, the construction supervisor for VWP, was put in charge of making sure everything went forward as expected, without any problems. He always tried to keep the boss happy.

*****

Meanwhile, Agent Ann Vern was back at the office, meticulously reading through the professor's notes. She was in search of more clues that might help her narrow down a suspect.

Ann read a letter addressed to Bill Archer from the professor that provided professional advice regarding the location of the new pipeline. The letter spoke about concerns with the VWP pipeline running through two extremely hazardous areas near the Appalachian Trail.

Hmm, so this must be what Steve was talking about. Gathering from what she'd just read, the pipeline would be installed in the middle of a very active Giles County Seismic Zone. She stopped to examine the details more closely. Perusing the professor's report aloud, "The US Forest Service has identified the steep slopes and landslide prone soils in the region as potential hazards during seismic activity." She understood how dangerous that could be should the soil ever become saturated. "Holy cow!"

According to Professor Brown's written notes and diagrams, he performed the research prior to addressing the public at the county meeting. Ann believed it was probable that the initial presentation included visual props. The minutes only paraphrased a portion of what the professor was trying to convey. Ann sat back in her chair. *I'm going to need to find out if there are any audio or video copies of the meeting. There's more to it than this. I just know it!*

Chapter 18 – Search for Omar

Ulysses Drum visited the *Chug it Down* bar and grill. He sat down at a hightop table and fumbled with his stubbly beard.

He wondered if Omar would be able to provide the evidence needed to shut down Merifrack. *Hmm, so Omar worked with Mr. Archer. But now Mr. Archer is missing… Jeez!*

Interrupting his train of thought, a slender brunette wearing a low cut blouse asked, "What are you drinking tonight, sweetie?"

"Bourbon on the rocks and a plate of your oysters, please." Ulysses knew he wouldn't be driving anywhere tonight. He'd already booked a room across the street at the Motel 10.

When she returned with his order, he politely thanked her and asked, "Could I ask you something?"

The waitress smiled at him. "Well, that depends on the question, I suppose."

"I'm looking for someone named Omar. I believe he lives here in town."

She tucked the empty round serving tray underneath her arm and tilted her head to the right slightly. Her pensive brown eyes drifted upward for a moment. "Omar, … Hmm… That name's not ringing a bell… Look, I only work Mondays and Wednesdays. It's quite possible someone else could've waited on him, especially if he came here on a weekend."

"I see. Perhaps you would know who works the weekend shift?"

"Ginger is your best bet."

"Thanks, um… What's your name?"

"Roxy."

"Thanks, Roxy. I'll check with Ginger tomorrow then."

Ulysses picked up his drink and enjoyed a few gulps. Then after he'd swallowed his last oyster, he felt vibrations in his back pocket. Anticipating it would be his wife, he abruptly walked out of the bar leaving Roxy a generous tip.

In the parking lot, he answered his phone. "Hello, darling! How's Tiffany doing tonight?"

Ulysses placed a hand on his forehead upon hearing the familiar play by play of what it took to soothe their colicky baby. "Well, at least she's sleeping now. You'll be able to get some rest. Listen, I've got to charge my phone; the battery never seems to last long whenever the temp drops. I'll give you a call tomorrow morning, okay?" It was true, he hadn't been able to charge the mobile and its battery life was subpar.

He felt guilty listening to her gripes and reassured her that he shouldn't need to be in Lycoming County for very long. He decided to leave out the part about overhearing people talk about a dead body. He didn't want his wife to worry. "I love you too. Sleep well, I'll be there as soon as I can."

When the conversation ended, he walked across the street, still pondering the day's events. Before drifting off to sleep that evening on a lumpy double bed, a thought remained with him. *I wonder if anyone ever reported that dead body?*

*****

The next morning, Ulysses rolled out of bed and pressed the on button of the tv's remote. Rubbing his eyes to focus better, he soon realized the question he'd asked himself was being answered on the early morning news.

"Jesus!" He turned up the volume and watched in disbelief. Aerial photos of Well Number 2 were being shown with a scrolling news ticker. The area was completely sectioned off with crime scene tape. A covered body was being hoisted into an ambulatory vehicle.

Ulysses felt cold and clammy. A chill lingered as he thought about yesterday. His pounding head was in sync with his heartbeat. It didn't take much longer for his stomach to join the orchestra. His body shook and there was no prolonging the inevitable. That's when he bolted to the bathroom. *Must've been those damned oysters.*

Opening the mini fridge, he snatched a ginger ale and took a few swigs. The fizzy cold beverage would soon quell the nausea, but it would not prevent him from ruminating about the dead body. What if the dead guy was Mr. Archer? He checked his messages again, half hoping he would discover Mr. Archer had returned back home safe and sound.

Hmm, perhaps Omar would be able to shed some light on this. After all, he was working with Mr. Archer. Ulysses was nervous about finding Omar. The last thing he wanted was to get caught up in any type of investigation. Ulysses was not the type to disobey direct orders; he wasn't about to start now. He needed this job to pay expenses and put food on the table.

If Ginger can't help me find Omar, I might need to contact Mrs. Archer. But that could get awkward. I'd feel obligated to help her find her husband. No, no, uh, uh, this is crazy. There's no way I'm getting involved!

Thursday after breakfast, he wandered into a local grocery store to ask around, but nobody knew Omar. Then he walked across the road into a barber shop. Nothing. By late morning, powerful storms moved through the area, forcing Ulysses to hunker down in his hotel room. On his laptop, he tried plugging Omar's name next to the town to see if any information popped up on the internet. Nobody named Omar had been listed in the entire county.

Ulysses hoped he'd have better luck asking Ginger about Omar this evening. Just after 4:00 p.m., he sauntered over to the bar. There were three vehicles in the parking lot. Pulling on the heavy wooden door, he quietly scooted inside, wiping his wet shoes on the interior doormat with the Budweiser logo. It was early; no customers had arrived yet. He sat down at the dimly lit bar and waited for someone to come out. He could hear a woman's hearty laughter in the back.

Five minutes later, a chunky middle aged woman stepped through the swinging doors as she was adjusting a waist apron. "Hello there! May I offer you a drink or something to eat?

Today's specials are right here." She handed him the standard drink menu with a short list of daily specials clipped to the front page.

"Sure, thanks. I'll have the sliders and a Coke." Ulysses figured he'd better order something before pumping anyone for information.

She immediately poured the soda and then left him alone to submit his order to the cook.

While Ulysses waited for his dinner, he noticed a television stuffed in the corner. CNN was on, but the volume was turned down. He could only read the rolling banners across the bottom of the screen. The dead person had not been named yet. *Probably because they need to notify the next of kin first.* He stuck the straw in his drink and sipped slowly, hoping the Coke would settle his nervous stomach.

Alas, his meal was delivered. Before the waitress returned to the kitchen, he mustered up the courage to ask for Ginger.

"You're looking at her!"

"When I spoke to Roxy last night, she said you'd be here tonight. I wanted to ask you… "

Ginger interrupted, "Look, before you go any further, Roxy called me last night. She mentioned some guy was looking for Omar. Are you a cop or something?"

Ulysses waved his hands in the air. "No! No, not even close. I work for the Environmental Protection Agency." He whipped out his work badge.

Ginger answered, "In that case, yeah, I've seen him around here a bunch of times. Quiet fellow, big brown eyes. He's usually with an elderly gentleman."

He softened his voice, "Would you know where I could find Omar?"

Ginger shrugged her shoulders and shook her head. "I'm afraid I don't know anything else about him."

He nodded and thanked her for her help. *Damn it! My only option now is to talk to Mrs. Archer.*

Leaving only a few fries and some smeared ketchup on the plate, he paid for the meal and added a $10.00 tip. Then he left the establishment.

Before it got too late, he knew he needed to talk to Mrs. Archer. He was dreading the thought of it. The acid in his stomach was churning again. He popped a couple of antacid tablets into his mouth. He had Bill Archer's home number programmed in his phone. *Let's get this over with.*

The phone rang several times before Mrs. Archer finally picked up. "Hello?"

"Hi, Mrs. Archer, my name is Ulysses Drum."

"I know exactly who you are! If it weren't for all of your meddling in the fracking business, my husband might still be alive!"

Ulysses did not anticipate the phone conversation would go like this. "Uh, I don't understand. What happened?"

"I just found out my husband's dead. Look, I'm not in the mood to discuss this with anyone! I always told Bill I didn't like the fact that he was using Omar to spy on Merifrack. Somebody found out and now my husband's dead!"

"Whoa, Mrs. Archer I'm sorry to hear about your husband's death. Really, ma'am, I cannot imagine how painful this must be for you. Please let me know if there's anything I can do for you." The words just came out of his mouth unexpectedly.

"I already told your boss; you'll have to contact Omar. He has the information you need. I don't know anything. Bill kept most of the details of his work to himself."

Hmm, so she'd already given Omar's name to Phil. That's weird! Why was he asking me for a name if he already knew? "Would you know where I could find Omar?"

"Why don't you ask his employer, Merifrack? I haven't spoken to Omar since my husband went missing. Now, I've answered all of your questions. Just leave me alone; I have nothing else to say to you." Mrs. Archer immediately hung up the phone.

Ulysses scrambled to the bench outside of the motel lobby and sat down. Staring off into space, he was attempting to absorb the shocking news. The knots in his stomach intensified. *Shit! So Omar has been working for Merifrack all this time while supplying Mr. Archer with evidence to permanently shut it down. Bill Archer must have been the dead guy on the news! This is unbelievable!*

The next thing he needed to do was contact his boss, Mr. Houlton. He hoped he might be able to get out of this mess. "Hi, Phil, weird thing is nobody seems to know where this Omar guy is. I just spoke with Mr. Archer's wife. On top of that, I just found out Mr. Archer is dead."

Hoping that would let him off the hook, Ulysses listened intently as his boss responded. Squeezing his eyes shut, Ulysses couldn't believe what he'd been told to do. "But, sir! That would be breaking and entering! Surely, you don't want me committing a crime."

Ulysses acknowledged his boss's concerns, "Yes, sir, I realize that Merifrack has been dodging the bullet, but wait…"

Clearly, his boss wanted him to retrieve the necessary evidence to take down Merifrack. When Ulysses's job position was threatened, he felt pushed up against a wall. "Yes, I know. They're screwing up the drinking water. Before this gets out of hand, I'll check around some more and see if I can find somebody who might be able to help us locate Omar. I'll be in touch."

After Ulysses hung up the phone, he let out a sigh. *I cannot believe my boss wants me to break into someone's home. Doesn't he realize how the system works? I'm more worried about the ramifications if I were to get caught breaking in.* He shuddered when he thought about the possible what ifs. He was especially concerned with how others might judge him, solely based on the color of his skin. His stomach churned again as he thought of his precious little daughter. *I refuse to put myself in that situation!*

He needed to hear his wife's voice. It went straight to voice mail. "Hi! It's me. I know I told you I wouldn't be here too long, but Mr. Houlton needs me to stay here until I can locate some guy in town named Omar. Apparently, he has enough evidence to shut down Merifrack for good. Anyway, talk to you later. Please give Tiffany my love. Love you too."

Glancing at his watch, it was too late to drive up to Merifrack tonight. He'd have to go first thing in the morning. Ulysses recalled what his boss had asked him to do. He couldn't help but wonder if anyone else in the department had ever been asked to break the law. He recalled the venomous tone of Mr. Houlton's voice. It sent shivers down his spine. It was obvious the head of the EPA wanted this evidence at any cost. *Why was it so important?*

*****

As Ulysses was driving up to Merifrack the next morning, the terrain became extremely steep. Suddenly, he noticed smoke rising from the front of his vehicle. The maintenance indicator lit up. "Probably the radiator, drat!" He pulled over, reached down and popped the hood. Donning protective gloves, he pressed the latch under the steaming hot hood and staked it open. Waving away a plume of hot steam, he made several attempts at contacting his motor club. His phone was unable to connect to a cell tower.

He remembered an unopened 12-pack of water bottles stashed behind the driver's seat. Pouring the contents of one into the radiator, he heard a sizzling noise. He suspected there was a leak, but didn't know how bad. He attempted to restart the engine, but the needle remained fixed on hot. Not wanting to damage his engine, he turned the ignition off.

A vehicle was approaching from behind. Ulysses waved his arms in the air, hoping it would stop.

Lo and behold, it was Morton Hendrix, the owner of Merifrack. But Ulysses noticed he was driving a different vehicle. This one was newer and in much better shape.

When it came to a complete stop, Morton stepped out of the vehicle and slammed the door shut.

Ulysses feigned a friendly smile. "Nice truck! In fact, I was looking at that model last week."

"You don't say! Well, this is my wife's truck. Mine is in the shop."

"Well, I was actually on my way up to see you."

Morton sarcastically asked, "Really? Did you find more violations?"

The last thing that Ulysses wanted was to insinuate that there was any trouble. He needed to obtain Omar's address, but did not want to cause suspicion. "I'm not here as an EPA inspector today. You see, I wanted to personally thank one of your employees for saving my life last night. Without his prompt intervention, I would have surely died."

While Morton was busy chomping on a toothpick, he spoke in his usual southern drawl. "Wow! And what did this person do to save your life?"

Ulysses continued with his story. "You see, I was having an allergic reaction and passed out before I could deploy my Epipen. He came to my rescue in the nick of time. I'd like to personally thank him."

Morton tossed the toothpick into a nearby wooded area. "Well, it's nice to know I have a hero working for me. Who are we talking about anyway?"

Ulysses carefully completed the tale. "I believe his first name was Omar. Someone had been kind enough to give it to me."

Morton replied, "Is that so? What a coincidence! I've been wondering where Omar might've gone. I guess he's too busy being a hero these days. Well, when you find him, please ask him to call me. I'd like to reward him for his good deed."

Ulysses remained calm. "Sure, I'd be happy to do that. Perhaps you have his address?"

"Sure, I'll look it up when we get to my office. Hop in! The cell service sucks out here. We'll get your truck towed to my mechanic. He's the best in town."

*****

Reexamining the piece of paper with Omar's address in his hand, Ulysses was sitting in the waiting room contemplating his next move.

One hour later, the radiator and water pump were replaced at the agreed upon price of $940.00. He felt lucky that the mechanic always kept an impressive supply of parts for the make and model of his truck. It was a popular vehicle driven by many locals.

Now it was time to drive to Omar's place. *I'll just see if he's home.*

Arriving at Ravenwood Lakes, Ulysses walked over to the far corner unit and tapped on the door. He didn't expect the door to move inward. He hesitated when he saw splintered wooden shards and debris from the broken jamb scattered on the ground. *Someone else has been here!*

It was around 2:30 in the afternoon. There was only one car in the parking lot, a good indication that most people were still at work. He reasoned with himself. *If Omar is in trouble, perhaps I could help? But what if somebody is dead in there. No, I better just contact the police.*

Just as Ulysses reached for his phone, he heard groaning noises.

Shouting loudly, "Hello! Is somebody in there?" He carefully pushed the door open with the tip of his sneaker.

"Mmm, mmm!" A young man was tied to a chair and his mouth was duct taped shut. He had a black eye and his face was swollen.

"Shit! What the hell happened?" Ulysses untied the man and removed the silver tape from his mouth.

"Ugh! Thanks. Two big guys broke into my apartment, beat me, and took my computer. Then they say leave, go back to Afghanistan."

Shaking his head in disbelief, "I'm guessing you are Omar."

Wide-eyed and frightened, Omar was hesitant to confirm at first. But his heart needed to trust somebody. He slowly nodded his head in reply.

"Whoa, man oh man! I've been looking all over for you. I'm Ulysses Drum. I work with the Environmental Protection Agency. Mr. Archer has been keeping us up to date on all of the fracking violations."

Omar broke down in tears. "Bill is my friend. Terrible what they did to him!"

"I take it, you heard about his death?"

He nodded. "The image of his body laid out on the ground will haunt me forever. Bill has a kind heart. How could somebody do that?"

Ulysses wanted to clarify. "Did you just say you saw Mr. Archer's dead body?"

"Yes, it's somebody at Merifrack. Probably knows we work together."

Ulysses had his phone at the ready. "I'd better contact the police."

"No! They say they come back and kill me!" Omar was visibly shaken. "Not safe here!"

"Okay, all right, … You can hang out with me for a little while. But, look, I've got a wife and kid. I don't want any trouble." Ulysses formed a soft spot for Omar's predicament.

"Thank you. Very kind of you…" Omar sank back down in the chair and placed his face in his hands. "Ohh, poor Mrs. Archer! She is so good to me. My heart is sad for her now. Perhaps I go check on her."

*****

Arriving at the Archers' home, Ulysses shifted his truck into park. "Omar, you go ahead. I'll just wait here."

Omar stared at Ulysses for a moment.

Ulysses confessed, "Trust me, I'm the last person she wants to see."

Ulysses watched Omar walk up the front porch stairs and knock on the door. When the door opened, Mrs. Archer threw her arms around Omar and wept. Ulysses wondered if he should let his boss know he found Omar. He dialed Phil's office number, but it went straight to voice mail. That's when he decided to hang up. *Ahh, forget about it. It's nothing that can't wait until I get back in town.* Then he leaned back the seat and folded his arms to get in a cat nap.

Chapter 19 – Karen Daisy

FBI Special Agent Karen Daisy was on assignment near El Paso, Texas. Working alongside fellow agents, trying to flush out the drug kingpin, Araña Malvado.

International intelligence sources in Mexico revealed that Araña had been arranging to move a large shipment of illegal drugs into the US. The FBI and CIA were working together at the southern border.

Hidden well behind some large trash receptacles, Karen was looking through night vision goggles. She watched CIA Agent Dave Zeller, under cover, dressed in street clothes. He was busy pretending to act like a person in despair, looking for his next fix.

The guise didn't take too long to draw the attention of a man wearing a backpack. Karen adjusted her goggles to get a clearer look.

The figure approached Zeller cautiously and dropped a small bag within six feet of him, then walked away. Karen followed the person who made the drop. He was standing caddy corner from her position, watching Zeller. She wondered if this guy was testing the waters.

The agents weren't interested in capturing a lone wolf. They needed to follow the supply chain. Karen whispered into a small microphone. "Zeller, camera's rolling…"

Zeller hobbled over to the bag and bent down slowly, retrieving the packet. Then he kneeled on the ground and pretended to take the substance. Continuing his performance, he swayed back and forth, chanting loudly.

Karen wanted to burst out laughing, but she maintained her composure, focusing on the man with the backpack.

Then a tall man wearing a hoodie entered her peripheral view. The whiskers from his coarse beard were poking out. "Well, what do we have here?" She panned over slightly and watched as this person was moving closer to Zeller.

"Heads up, Zeller, a man with a hoodie is coming up behind you on your left." *What's happening here?* Karen wondered if this man had been looking for drugs. The man skirted past Zeller and sauntered up to the figure with the backpack. They both moved out of her line of sight. "Damn-it!" A large group of saguaro cacti blocked her vision. *Crap!* "Can anybody tell me what's happening? I've lost my visual." *Shit!*

CIA Special Agent Griff Whistler was able to view the pair before they disappeared into an abandoned building. "They just entered the *Lucky Duck*." Agent Whistler was a reliable counterpart. His commitment to the job for over fifteen years was admirable.

Karen knew exactly where she needed to reposition herself. Dressed in all black to camouflage, she darted across an adjacent alleyway and wedged herself behind another dumpster, keeping her vision locked on the entrance of the old arcade that still glowed underneath bright neon lights.

Rear access to the building had been secured with metal roll downs when Karen canvassed the area earlier that day. Curious why the front entrance had not been locked up accordingly, there wasn't much time to dwell on this observation. She watched the glass door open. The person with a backpack reemerged and seemed distracted, fishing through his backpack.

Oblivious to his surroundings, he headed in her direction. She immediately leaned back, letting the lightweight goggles hang around her neck. She was completely hidden behind the large garbage receptacle. Closing her eyes, she focused on her breath, trying not to purge the contents of her stomach as a foul odor hung in the dense air.

Approaching footsteps stopped for several minutes. There was a loud belch followed by the noise of an empty aluminum can being dropped onto the asphalt. He must have kicked it because it ricocheted off a nearby wall. Karen watched the soda can roll and creep to a stop when it struck her left boot. Her heartbeat was racing. She lifted the Glock 19M out of her holster, hoping she wouldn't be forced to use it.

The footsteps resumed and he was whistling a tune. After he passed by the dumpsters where she was hidden in the shadows, she returned her gun to its holster and picked up the night vision goggles. It was apparent he was wearing a pair of earbuds, listening to music.

She proceeded to follow him down the alley, staying well out of his sight range.

Meanwhile, Agent Whistler repositioned himself to face the only egress point of the old arcade building, waiting for the tall man with the beard.

In the wee hours of the morning, agents stood by their posts, surrounding the building.

Karen was the only agent in motion covering the suspect with the backpack. She eventually watched him enter a modest single family home. She immediately spoke into her hidden microphone. "Suspect entered the dwelling's basement. I'm sending the info." An encrypted location ping was sent to fellow agents. Continuous surveillance on all possible leads needed to be established.

Karen needed to get some sleep after working a double shift. She briefed the next team of agents and returned to the motel where she was staying under the name of Jane Parker.

*****

For four days, agents monitored all suspicious activity in the area. It was odd that two people entered but only the one with a backpack exited the old arcade.

CIA Agent Whistler and two field agents donned bulletproof vests and helmets. They entered the building, unsure of what they would encounter.

Flashlights revealed graffiti walls and chewing gum lined concrete floors. All that remained were five abandoned pinball machines and one Pac-Man unit. There was no other way out of this place, so where did the tall person go?

Agent Whistler suspected they were missing something. He looked closer at the arcade games. When his hip accidentally bumped into the corner of the bulky Pac-Man machine, it moved easily on rollers. *Hmm, that's strange, I don't ever remember these things having wheels.* He pushed the boxy contraption out of the way and noticed there was a square hole underneath. It was large enough for a person to fit inside, but they needed to be careful.

A technical crew of experts followed up by sending down a robotic dog equipped with a camera, but they did not gather much data due to the tunnel being booby-trapped. Clearly, someone covered his tracks.

*****

Agent Karen Daisy was back on another long shift. She had been waiting for an opportunity to explore the home where the person with a backpack entered the basement. Using heat surveillance equipment, she determined the elderly gentleman was home alone.

The air was cool and the skies darkened with storm clouds. Rain was spitting. *Perfect!* She was fully hidden under a large navy raincoat, with the hood up. With search warrant in hand, she approached the home and knocked on the door.

Rammi Finjaven slowly opened the door. "Hello. Can I help you?"

She introduced herself and flashed a badge. Then she handed him a copy of the search warrant.

Rammi politely answered all of the standard questions. But when the questioning seemed targeted at Ramon, he asked, "Is he in some trouble?"

"The FBI has witnessed suspicious activity in the area. We need to follow up on some leads. Could I take a look around?"

He seemed happy to cooperate. "Of course, but Ramon has only key to basement."

"May I?" She pulled out her lock picking device.

Rammi beamed, "Oooh, like Hollywood movie!"

Karen was a pro at picking locks. She inserted the tool and jiggled the lock. It gracefully opened. *Voila!*

He offered to accompany Karen to the basement, but when she refused, he responded, "Okay, no problem…" He respected the fact that she was packing heat.

She donned plastic gloves and descended the staircase.

A twin bed with a wicker headboard was neatly made. She carefully inspected the mattress, sheets, pillows, blankets, and puffy yellow quilt. She observed no visible signs of drug paraphernalia. The room was tidy. Nothing seemed out of place. Only the top drawer of a tall bureau contained clothing. She inventoried three pairs of boxers, two green work shirts, one pair of black pants, one undershirt and two pairs of socks. Each item of clothing was neatly folded. The rest of the four drawers were empty. *Well, one thing's for sure, this guy doesn't own much.*

Turning on her flashlight, she methodically looked underneath and behind the bed and then walked over to a small desk that had been positioned in front of dramatic floor-to-ceiling velvety curtains in deep burgundy. She parted the curtains to provide extra lighting. As she peaked behind the desk, she noticed a dusty, half mangled bottle cap and something else wedged behind the desk. "Hmm, what's this?"

When she lifted up the lightweight object, she realized it was the backpack. She carefully examined each compartment and found a folded printout of a flight itinerary issued by United Airlines. The nonstop flight would be leaving El Paso tomorrow morning, arriving in Washington Dulles in the afternoon. She quickly took a photo of it before returning it to the backpack. Other than a well-used chapstick, there was nothing else in the bag. She grumbled to herself, "Dang it!"

As she was returning everything to its original place, she wondered if perhaps the bearded man had given him the ticket. *Hmm,… but why Washington?*

Rammi interrupted her train-of-thought. He cleared his throat. "I hope everything, uh, okay down there. I make us tea."

She answered his question as she climbed the staircase. "Yes, everything is fine."

Locking the basement door, Karen entered the kitchen. A table had been set and Rammi pulled out a chair for her. A cozy wrapped ceramic teapot was steeping a few bags of Typhoo tea. Rammi was very particular about his tea. He preferred only the best British tea.

Karen sat down with him. "Thank you."

Rammi wanted to help. "No problem… As you know, America is my home now."

Karen asked in a kind, soothing voice. "Did Ramon ever tell you he would be traveling to Washington DC?"

He shook his head in reply. "No, no, Ramon have no money for travel. He must stay here and work."

Karen asked another question. "Do you know if he has any family in Washington DC?"

Rammi confidently answered, "No, family in Venezuela."

Nothing was making any sense. She suspected Rammi didn't know anything about Ramon's plans. She decided it was best to finish her cup of tea and depart. "Rammi, I've only just met you, but you seem like a nice man. I'm going to offer some friendly advice. Be careful what you say around Ramon. He could be involved with dangerous people."

Frightened, Rammi asked, "Should I worry?"

Karen replied, "It's difficult to say for sure, but if I were you, I definitely wouldn't mention anything about the search. It might trigger a bad reaction."

The last thing Rammi wanted was to jeopardize his son's future. "No problem..." Then he made a gesture that looked like he was zipping his lips closed.

Returning to her surveillance team, she shared her findings.

Karen knew she'd be traveling back to Washington DC tomorrow. She decided to contact Ann Vern. Her call went straight to voice mail. "Ann, just called to chat. Give me a call when you get a chance. Ciao!" It was always the same standard message, but rarely did it ever mean they would chit chat about anything. It usually involved a case that required a fresh pair of eyes.

Chapter 20 – Trail Blazers

March 18th

Agent Carter Bixben promised to give the Langford sisters some space. They began the northbound journey early in the morning at Mile Marker 1016.6 (Loudoun Heights, Virginia).

The girls were in deep conversation, averaging a fast pace of between 3 and 4 miles per hour, they lost track of the time. Rarely taking breaks, they slowed down to rehydrate and snack on granola bars. Determined to keep going, they hiked much more than they'd originally anticipated.

Peggy could see that the sun was setting. "According to my map program, there's a shelter up ahead." They initially planned to go 20 miles, but changed their minds when they encountered light foot traffic and perfect weather. The peace and quiet was the best medicine to melt away the stress.

*****

After arriving at Ensign Cowall Shelter, Melody joined her sister on a picnic bench. They had the place to themselves. Changing into some breathable Crocs, they laid out their boots and sweaty socks to dry out. "Can you really believe it, Peggy? We hiked 33.5 miles in one day!"

Peggy responded, "Hey, that's more than a marathon. I guess all our training really paid off."

Melody was massaging her feet. "We are so lucky they assigned us Carter Bixben. Don't you think he is adorable, not to mention sweet as pie?"

Peggy stood up and stretched her calves and hamstrings. "Melody, if I didn't know any better, I'd say you were crushing on the guy."

Melody lightly bit her bottom lip to hold back from smiling. Then she responded, "And what if I was? Come on, is that such a bad thing?"

Peggy was stretching her arms overhead. "Nope, but he might already be taken."

Melody placed both hands on each side of her waist. "And what makes you think that?"

The conversation abruptly ended when they heard approaching footsteps. They pulled two tents out of the packs and walked over to a raised dirt platform. The girls were just starting the assembly process when Agent Bixben arrived.

"I'm glad to see you've decided to camp here for the night. I checked the radar. The wind's supposed to pick up later tonight. It might even rain. Cold front… I'll set up my sleeping capsule."

Peggy snickered and whispered to Melody, "It looks more like a nylon coffin to me."

Melody blushed and shushed her sister.

They watched his muscular body wriggle inside with a backpack.

Melody was still grinning at Carter's capsule comment. She announced, "We'll be back in a jiffy. Gonna gather more water."

Agent Bixben nodded and waved his hand. "Sure thing…" His feet were throbbing and he was feeling exhausted. He didn't want to admit that it had been over a year since he'd done any long hikes. The day to day tasks at the White House didn't exactly prepare him for this. He knew deep down that the job should never be an excuse for slacking on his fitness routine.

Peggy was first to spot a small toilet shed. Less than a quarter mile away, there was a clean water source to refill the canteens and wash up. They clipped the canteens onto the metal rungs of their belts so their hands would be free to gather kindling and firewood.

Returning to the campsite, they placed the wood kindling and some larger pieces near a rock-lined fire pit. Feeling tired, intense hunger pangs pushed them to keep going.

Melody's polite nature prompted her ask, "Hey, Carter, you eating anything tonight?

We're going to boil some water for tea and dinner."

Bixben responded, "Okay, thanks. Sounds good. I'll be out in a minute." He finished bandaging his blisters accordingly and slid on some lightweight thermal slippers.

Melody nestled small, dry pieces of wood around a fire starter, then lit it with a match. Before long, a hot fire was going. Soon enough the smaller branches caught fire and it wouldn't be long before they added larger logs. They found a rusty grate and placed it over the heat source. It was sufficient for placing their metal containers full of water. Opening up a couple of dehydrated meal boxes, they poured steaming water over top to reconstitute, stirring with a spork.

Mouthwatering aromas drifted toward Carter's tent. He unzipped his tent and scooted out. "That smells amazing!"

Melody asked, "Carter, where's your dinner?"

Carter pulled out a couple of granola bars. "Right here." He didn't want to tell the girls he'd forgotten to add meals to his backpack.

Melody reached into her backpack. "Nonsense, here I brought an extra meal." Melody lifted out a pasta dinner package. She opened it and poured the hot water over top stirring it for him.

Carter swallowed hard. "Wow! Uh, thanks, Melody. That's very kind of you!"

When Peggy witnessed Carter interacting with her sister, she believed there was a real connection. She wondered if perhaps she had been wrong about him.

*****

Just as Carter had predicted, the wind picked up. All boots and gear were stored inside the tents for the night.

The fire dwindled down to glowing ashes. Cool air mixed with rainfall reduced the chances of the fire reigniting.

Melody was excited about what tomorrow's adventure might hold. Before tonight, she never admitted to anyone that she had a crush on Carter. It would have been completely inappropriate, especially during her mother's Presidency.

Peggy's voice was just barely audible over the wind, "Let's refill our canteens again tomorrow morning before breakfast. Well, good night, Melody!"

"Yes, good idea…Night!" Melody zipped up her sleeping bag and placed her hands behind her head. Her heart was in overdrive thinking about Carter.

*****

Day two, the girls were getting close to their pre-planned destination, just south of the Mason-Dixon Line on the AT, they stopped to recheck the digital map on Peggy's phone.

Melody was sad. "Peggy, I'm having so much fun. The time went by too quickly. I really wish we could hike more. I'm going to miss this. It's so beautiful and serene!" That wasn't the only reason why she wanted to stay longer. She was hoping for an excuse to spend more time with Carter.

Peggy made a suggestion. "Maybe we could go a little further into Pennsylvania." She double checked her phone. "Aha, there's a Walmart 2.1 miles away from here in Waynesboro, Pennsylvania."

Peggy announced, "You know, we'll have to clear it with Bixben." Melody's heart skipped a beat when she heard her sister say his name.

Melody responded, "Great! Let's run it by him. He should be here shortly."

Five minutes later, Carter Bixben walked up to the pair. He exclaimed, "Can you believe it. We're almost there! Wow, forty-three miles in two days!"

"Melody and I were having a conversation. We'd really like to walk farther into Pennsylvania. I found a place, not far from here, where we can resupply." Peggy was hoping he would be on board with the new plan.

Carter ran a hand through his wavy dark hair, and sighed. "Look, I don't think that's a good idea. You girls know the security protocols; everything has to be pre-planned in advance."

Peggy's Type A personality came out. "Look, we'll take full responsibility. Just make a phone call and tell them the new schedule. We'll stay at the Deer Lick Shelters tonight, it's less than five miles from here. It shouldn't be a big deal. Please! If we just add four more days to the trip, we promise to stop wherever that takes us."

Carter sighed, "All right, but I'll have to contact Flex before we do anything." He turned on his satellite phone and made the call.

The girls had originally prepared to take the extra time off from work to recuperate from the hike. The only person they needed to contact was their mother. They figured she might want to hear how the hike was going anyway.

Peggy turned on her mobile phone. "Mom, guess what,… We're going to add four more days to our trip. We love it out here in the wilderness."

"That's wonderful! Four more days, wow! Have you seen any wildlife?"

Melody giggled, "Only if you count hikers. Oh, and a couple of squirrels."

Chapter 21 – Flashback

Isaad Dil learned of Jackson Troy's death as a result of a suicide bomber shortly after arriving in Langley, Virginia. He couldn't believe the grim news. He'd only spoken to his dear friend less than 24 hours prior to arrival in the United States.

*****

Several months had passed since that chaotic date of arrival into the United States. Isaad was feeling guilty for not speaking up about the man who threatened his son. The Dil family was relieved when Abdul disappeared, never to be seen again.

Isaad kept having flashbacks of Abdul staring intensely at his family during the evacuation process into the United States. The gun that threatened Taji's life was apparently never discovered among the chaos. Isaad never doubted for a minute that Abdul could access it. Even after all of this time, Isaad broke into a sweat whenever he thought about the incident. He wiped his brow with his sleeve. If the military ever found out about the lie, Isaac was certain it would lead to a hefty prison sentence.

Chapter 22 – Murder Victims

Agent Vern set up Professor Brown's computer. She placed the bulging folder of pipeline data next to it, hoping to piece together more clues.

Ann wondered - *What did these people all have in common?* She thumbed through the stack of murder victims once again. Ann rolled out a large dry erase board and picked up a marker. Scribbling away, she needed to establish a possible motive.

She found trail nicknames for 5 of the 22 total victims. *Professor Arthur Brown* was placed in the first column of the first row, since he was believed to be the first victim. The remaining headings were titled: *Job/Pol. Party*, *Trail Nickname*, and *Region*. She filled in the data for all remaining victims, saying each aloud to herself, hoping to cement the facts in her brain, *"Professor, Democrat, 'Brown Bear', West Virginia…"*

The blue marker squeaked as she continued, *"Mark Wickham, attorney, Democrat, 'Turtle Man', West Virginia..."*

Ann inhaled deeply as she moved to the next row. Writing as quickly and neatly as she could, she grumbled to herself, *"Catie Minnow, software engineer, Democrat, 'Meta Key', Pennsylvania..."*

Jotting down more victims, Ann left most of the nickname slots blank. She knew she would need to contact the ranger to find out which nicknames belonged to which victims. When she got down to the last two victims, she sighed before saying, *"Joel Taginaw, geologist, Democrat, Virginia, Jim Dennis..."*

"Wait a minute!" She paused, putting the marker down. *He was the 22nd victim.* She sat on the corner of the conference table. Placing both hands behind her head, she remembered he was the *pastor*. But that wasn't the only thing. "Hmm, he's the only Republican on this list. But he was friends with Joel Taginaw." She circled the two and connected them with arc arrows. "Trail name, *'Lego Man'...*" Ann recalled interviewing the pastor's wife who mentioned about his enthusiasm with Legos.

Agent Vern wondered if Mr. Dennis's relationship with Taginaw made him a target. *Perhaps whoever did this was targeting Democrats.* "No, there has to be more to this. *Maybe* the pastor was in the wrong place at the wrong time."

Ann's last thought... *The bodies were all discovered along remote portions of the trail.*

It was getting late and she needed to head home. She abbreviated a note to herself on a *Post-It* note. *'Follow up HP ranger.'*

*****

At home, Ann made herself a pot of tea and settled down in a plush recliner. She flipped on the reading lamp positioned overhead and read through the first five pages of the *Pipeline Public Meeting Minutes*. Then she was startled by a whistling noise. *Ahh, tea time!*

Reading another ten pages of the fifty-something page document, she couldn't hold back a yawn.

Ann poured herself another mug of strong tea and thought, *Boy, if I ever have trouble falling asleep, I'll just read this shit.*

Trying to ignore the obvious typos along the way, Ann highlighted the names of each person who spoke at the meeting about the pipeline issue. This would make it much easier to focus on what each person said.

Annoyed with the lack of detail surrounding what seemed like critical parts of the meeting, she huffed. "Unbelievable! The stenographer just paraphrased. No names have been included here. Drat! I'll have to find out if they have a recording of that meeting. I've got to find out who these so-called *members of the public* were." Frustrated, she tucked the document back into the file.

*****

The next morning, Ann immediately contacted the Giles County Clerk's Office, who hosted the multi-county meeting. "Yes, this is FBI Special Agent Vern; I'm hoping you have an audio copy of the pipeline public hearing that you can share with me."

The clerk on the other end responded, "Yes, we record all of our meetings. It usually takes about one week and costs $10.00 for a copy. We now accept PayPal."

Ann asked, "Is there any way it can be expedited?"

The girl placed her on hold for several minutes. "Yes, for an extra two bucks, I can send it out by the end of the day."

Ann was agreeable to those terms and provided her email, "That's fair, would you please send me the county's payment link?"

As promised, Ann received a digital copy of the invoice, including all payment options. *Works for me!*

*****

Ann phoned the Appalachian Trail Conservancy.

A girl with a squeaky voice answered.

Ann introduced herself, mentioning that she was an FBI agent. She asked to speak to the ranger in charge.

"That would be Glenn Flip. But he isn't here today. He comes in four days a week."

Ann asked, "What is your name? Perhaps you might be able to assist."

"Margaret… Sure, I'd be happy to help."

"How would I be able to obtain a copy of hiker registrations within a specific time frame?"

Margaret answered, "Oh, I'm sorry. Nobody is allowed to see that information. It's kept confidential. But anyone can come in person to view our log book with trail nicknames."

Ann sighed. "Yes, of course, I understand. But I'm not just anyone. Surely Mr. Flip could allow that information to be shared with the FBI."

Margaret hesitated, "I'm not supposed to give that information out."

Ann closed her eyes. This girl was trying her patience. "I understand, but in certain circumstances, wouldn't the FBI be permitted to obtain a copy of that list?"

Margaret answered, "My boss keeps a copy in his computer, but we are never allowed to give it out to anyone. It would have to be an emergency situation, but only Glenn could make a decision like that."

Ann rolled her eyes and tapped the back of her pen on a notepad. "I see. And what would Glenn consider as an emergency situation?"

Margaret offered a couple of scenarios, "Um, like a missing person case or maybe an escaping prisoner."

Ann coughed, trying to suppress her laughter. She knew that an escaping prisoner would never take such a risk. "When will Mr. Flip be returning?"

Margaret paused for several seconds. "Tomorrow morning…"

When the phone call ended, Ann contacted Steve. "Steve! How would you feel about going on another field trip with me?"

Agent Flex was curious. "Where are we going this time?"

"Back to Harpers Ferry to meet with the ranger. Apparently, he keeps a list of names on a database. But he'll only share this information if we flash our badges."

Steve snickered. "Flashing has never been an issue for me."

Ann smirked, "Ha! Good to know. I'll have to remember that."

Steve cleared his throat. "But seriously, it is ironic that you mentioned Harpers Ferry. I just got off the phone with a fellow agent who's hiking just north of that area. How about I pick you up tomorrow at 7 a.m.? Will that work?"

"Sounds good. Tomorrow it is." Ann exhaled with a smile after the conversation ended. She loved Steve's humor.

Chapter 23 – The List

Glenn Flip was indeed on duty. He was busy assisting a group of southbound hikers.

Agents Flex and Vern surveyed the station. They noticed an empty office in the back corner. As they got closer, Ann whispered in Steve's ear, "Look, I'll bet that's the ranger's office. The door's ajar! Anyone could just wander in without even being seen."

Steve responded, "Uh huh, well that's interesting. You might be right about that."

While waiting, they browsed through the log book with nicknames. The only information that could be useful here were the dates when hikers signed in.

Agent Vern used her phone to snap photos of only those who'd signed in within the date ranges of the murders. She included adjacent pages, hoping not to exclude anyone that could provide more answers.

Something else caught Ann's attention. "Steve, would you look at that!"

"What?"

"Some of the same nicknames reappear more than once on different dates."

"Hmm, maybe they were weekend warriors establishing an exercise routine."

Placing an index finger on her chin, "Dunno, but I am curious about it."

Glenn Flip finished giving directions to the hikers and was busy tidying up a stack of disarranged maps.

Ann nudged Steve with her elbow. "Let's go see what Mr. Flip can tell us."

They formally introduced themselves after flashing the appropriate identification badges. Agent Vern made a suggestion. "Mr. Flip, would it be possible to discuss this matter privately?"

"Yes, please come this way." He showed them to the small office. It had stacks of maps, multiple guidebooks on the Harpers Ferry area, and a collection of old log books.

Just before he closed the door, Ranger Flip announced to his assistant, "Margaret, please take over for me and hold all my calls."

Mr. Flip offered them two chairs and then sat down in his antique wooden rolling chair. "Forgive the mess, we are in the process of archiving our files."

Ann led with the fact that they were working on a case involving a series of mysterious deaths. "Mr. Flip, we'll need to find out the trail names for this list of victims." She pushed a paper containing 17 names. "If you could tell us what their trail names were and when they registered."

Agent Flex added, "And how often they registered."

Mr. Flip replied, "Let me see what I can do. Printer's on the fritz, so I'll have to email it to you."

"That's fine, thank you. Here is my direct email."

After confirming receipt, Ann asked, "Mr. Flip, has anyone else requested this information?"

"No, ma'am, not in the past year anyway… And those were for missing kids."

Steve placed his right hand on the top of his head in a pensive fashion. "Mr. Flip, I hope you don't take this inquisition the wrong way, but does your establishment have proper security protocols in place to thwart hacks and cyber attacks?"

"I wish. No, in fact, after our system got hacked, we hired a computer technician to upgrade the security system."

Agent Vern leaned forward. "I see. And how long ago did this happen?"

Mr. Flip cleared his voice. "About five or six months ago, but I don't recall the exact date."

Ann asked, "Did you report this hacking incident?"

His voice lowered, "Well, uh, you see. No, I never reported it. I figured it was no big deal since we didn't lose anything important."

Ann clicked her ballpoint pen and flipped open her notepad. "I see. Uh, may I please have the name of the person who is updating your computer system?"

"Samuel Regis… But he's away on a two-week vacation, doing some hiking on the Appalachian Trail. I believe he has been blogging on *Trail Journals*."

Ann leaned in. "Okay. Mr. Flip, would you happen to have a way I could get in touch with Mr. Regis?"

"Yes, here is his business card. But you might have to keep trying. Cell service on the trail is sketchy."

Agent Flex was curious, "One more thing before we go… My partner noticed the log book out front was filled in many times by the same people, but on different dates. Certainly, these can't be thru-hikers."

"Oh, yes! Those people volunteer and maintain the trail. We ask that they sign the log book for safety reasons. I keep a separate database just for those volunteers."

Ann nodded, "Would you please send me that list as well?"

"Sure thing…"

*****

Returning to her office later that day, Agent Vern was pleasantly surprised when she saw a small package had arrived via express mail from the Giles County Clerk's Office. *Well, that was fast!*

Upon opening the manilla envelope, she slid out a dvd encased in clear plastic, labeled 'Pipeline Meeting'. Since it was a video of the entire event, she hoped it would be more entertaining than reading the lackluster minutes.

Pressing the ejection button on the side of her laptop, a thin tray popped out. After inserting the disk, her eyes remained glued to the computer screen.

She intended to watch it from beginning to end, jotting down all important details. During parts of the meeting, tensions escalated. Ann turned up the volume and replayed some scenes more than once.

'The bottom of the slope is full of karst, or limestone. This 42-inch pipeline would be under enormous pressure, 1,440 pounds per square inch to be exact.'

Ann watched another drama unfold on the dvd:

{Professor Brown was acting livid. "That's an explosion waiting to happen!"

Martin Drawbuck shook his head in disbelief. "Nonsense! Mr. Brown, you don't know what you're talking about!"

Professor Brown slammed his fist down on the podium. "No? Perhaps you forgot about that 20-inch pipeline explosion in Sissonville, West Virginia back in December of 2012. It was so intense, that it melted part of Interstate 77."

Martin chuckled and waved his hand in a dismissive way. "I assure you, we have put in all the necessary safety protocols."}

After the meeting adjourned, Ann wanted to learn more about Martin Drawbuck. She needed to cover all bases and decided to add him to the suspects list.

Chapter 24 – At the Coal Mine

When Adam arrived at the job site on his bicycle at ten minutes to six in the morning, he witnessed Abdul rearranging items on his truck bed. Although Adam was only 14 years old, he was a good judge of character. There was something about Abdul that didn't sit well with him.

Abdul hadn't realized anyone was watching him. He pulled a tarp back over the remaining contents and threw a knapsack over his left shoulder.

Adam walked toward the entrance to the mine. He adjusted the elastic band on his safety goggles and fitted a miner's hardhat to his head. Then he wore a respirator apparatus to reduce exposure to pollutants. He lowered himself down a vertical man shaft. He didn't bother to wait for Abdul. He just wanted to get to work.

*****

Over the next few months, Abdul kept busy stockpiling supplies in his home to build bombs. Each tightly sealed canister contained enough explosives to take out an entire city block. His goal was to move over one thousand of the explosives into the mine shaft using his pickup truck. He arrived well before his coworkers, discretely transporting multiple truckloads of these deadly explosives.

Abdul used two large rolling suitcases to transport the canisters to an abandoned section of the mine shaft. After studying a map of the geological region and the major fault lines, Abdul concentrated on one area in particular. It was a specific seismic hazard zone with a conglomeration of overlapping tectonic plates. This meant that extreme explosive forces would most likely trigger violent earthquakes and landslides, rupturing underground pipelines and causing massive destruction and loss of life.

Once all of the cans were stacked in place, Abdul could focus on programming the timer. His goal was almost complete.

Chapter 25 – Dulles Airport

Undercover agents on board Flight 232 were tailing Ramon Blanco. The kid moved quickly. He only had one backpack, yet agents scrambled to keep tabs on him among a dense group of college students. Ramon didn't even realize he was being followed.

The crowded airport made it extremely difficult for agents to maneuver. Twenty minutes later, they were flabbergasted when they suddenly realized they were following another man, wearing an identical hoodie.

*****

Karen Daisy's flight finally arrived in Washington Dulles three hours after Ramon's arrival. By the time she turned her phone back on and discovered the screwup, she cursed out loud. Nearby passengers gave her a nasty look.

The sun would be setting in a few hours and Karen knew that Ramon could have gone anywhere. She sent out necessary cell phone alerts and photos asking for people to contact the FBI if anyone sees this person.

Once she exited the plane, she contacted her friend and colleague, Ann Vern, about the incident. "I cannot believe this guy just disappears into thin air. I feel like all of our time has been wasted. Oh, it's so frustrating!"

Ann offered some sound advice, "Put yourself in his shoes. I would imagine that he also received the alert, like everyone else. He will be forced to go into hiding. Think about places where he could avoid people."

Karen thought about it. "You're right… Perhaps he is hiding in the wilderness somewhere. Who knows, maybe he decided to hike the Appalachian Trail."

"Anything's possible, I suppose."

Chapter 26 – Gunshots

Bang! Bang!

"Gunshots! Get down!" Peggy shouted at Melody.

The girls crouched down in a densely wooded area where they huddled together. Rapidly breathing, they could just barely see the trail.

Melody whispered, "Peggy, I'm worried about Carter. He's usually right behind us."

For the next several minutes, the Langford sisters remained still and listened. Sounds of cool breezes and rustling leaves were mixed with songbirds. Nature was returning to its former state.

"Peggy, I think we need to backtrack and find Carter. Something's not right, what if something bad happened?" Melody swallowed, feeling anxious.

Peggy knew her sister was right. They needed to verify that Bixben was okay. "Let's go back, but not on the main trail. We need to keep out of sight to avoid becoming an easy target."

Melody nodded in agreement.

Because the terrain was not worn in, the girls needed to slow down at times and carefully navigate through the untamed wilderness. Climbing over large rock formations, they kept stopping to check their surroundings.

A field of slippery moss covered boulders mixed with hidden tree roots made it more hazardous, but they managed to work their way through. Occasionally, they paused to hide behind larger rocks to make sure nobody was around. All of their senses were on hyper alert.

Peggy warned her sister, "Look out for rattlesnakes! This is where they're more likely to hide."

"Terrific, first gunshots, now rattlesnakes... Oh, joy." Melody sarcastically commented under her breath.

They heard a muffled cry. "Ahhh! Help!"

The girls looked at each other.

Peggy pointed, "It's coming from over there." When she saw her sister stand up she cautioned her, "Wait, Melody, what if it's a trap?"

Melody paused for a moment to look back at her sister. "But what if it's Carter?"

Peggy pointed uphill, "Let's get a better view of the surrounding area first. Then we can approach from over there."

"Whatever! I'll take my chances." Melody risked her own personal safety to help whoever it might be.

Peggy reached the top of the hill and viewed Bixben laying on the ground. He was holding his left side. His hands were covered in blood.

Peggy sprinted down the hill to join Melody, "Oh my God, Bixen's been shot!"

Carter Bixben was fading in and out of consciousness.

Melody saw the agent's satellite phone in multiple pieces near Carter. "Peggy, call 9-1-1 on your phone!" She was certified in CPR and instinctively removed her bulky olive hoodie and wrapped it snuggly around Bixben's bleeding torso to try and stop the bleeding.

While Melody was working on Carter, Peggy made several attempts at reaching Secret Service Agent Steve Flex. Her mobile phone was having difficulty connecting to a cell tower.

*****

When Peggy's phone call finally went through, Flex picked up immediately. "Peggy, is everything all right?" He knew she wouldn't be calling him if it wasn't urgent.

Peggy's breathing was erratic. "No, Agent Bixben's been shot! He's bleeding. Melody's trying to stop the bleeding. He's already lost so much blood. His satellite phone has been broken into pieces. Can you find our location using my phone? I'm not exactly sure where we are."

Flex was urgently trying to trace her signal. "Stay on the line, Peggy I'm…"

When the phone call dropped, Peggy looked down at her phone. "Shit!" A revolving sunburst indicated that her phone was searching for a signal. "This cannot be happening!"

Peggy tried climbing back up the hill, away from the interference of the trees. Focused on her phone, she was trying to get a signal.

*****

When Peggy dropped off the grid and could not be found, Agent Flex tried tracing Agent Bixben's satellite phone to see if he could determine its last transmission point prior to the accident.

Narrowing down the last known position, Flex zoomed in on a tiny circle blinking on the screen. He shouted, "Bingo! Got it!"

Flex immediately contacted first responders to request medical assistance and then sent the coordinates to other agents in the area. Finally, Flex notified his boss, Deputy Director Edward Phloeb.

Steve Flex and Ann Vern left the Appalachian Trail Conservancy and rushed to the SUV. A prompt decision had been made to do some off-roading on uncharted, overgrown service roads. The ride was bumpy, to say the least, but they remained steadfast and determined. Their only chance at finding the girls was to follow the little blinking dot.

Ann shouted, "Turn left! Looks like it'll take us to an old logging road."

Meanwhile, Phloeb was organizing a team of agents to meet up with Agent Flex and bring home the former President's daughters.

*****

A medical helicopter flew into the Peters Mountain Wilderness, Pennsylvania. A dense canopy of trees made it difficult to pinpoint Agent Bixben's exact location.

When Melody heard the helicopter, she grabbed the satellite phone's shattered glass screen and ran into an open area. Then she faced it toward the sun and moved it back and forth so it would reflect the sunlight.

It worked! The helicopter pilot lowered the vessel into a wide clearing. A crew of medical personnel dragged a stretcher and some gear and followed Melody to the unconscious body.

Paramedics could see that Carter Bixben's pallor was pale. He'd lost a lot of blood. His pulse was weak and breathing was strained.

Melody watched them place an oxygen mask over his nose and mouth. She knelt down and placed both hands over her mouth. She helplessly watched as the paramedics continued working on Bixben. Not wasting any time, they maneuvered his body onto the stretcher and rolled him toward the waiting chopper.

Melody ran behind the stretcher, tears streamed down her face. Not knowing if he could hear her, she clenched her stomach in agony and shouted, "Carter! Come back to me. I need you! I love you!"

After the helicopter took off, Melody felt shaky. She searched for her sister. "Peggy! Peggy, where the hell are you?"

Chapter 27 – Langford Sisters

After engaging the emergency brake, Steve and Ann exited their vehicle.

Steve double checked his phone and then pointed to the left. "Over there!"

Ann followed behind closely, keeping an eye on where she was stepping. There were so many loose rocks and large roots. It would be easy to twist an ankle out here. She came to a screeching halt when she overheard voices. It was a conversation between two hikers. She reached out and tapped Steve on his left shoulder.

When Steve saw her place an index finger in front of her lips, he realized she must have heard something. He gave her a puzzled look, curious about what she was listening to. His range of hearing was not as proficient as hers.

Ann detected a high pitched, crackly female voice. The lady was speaking to a male with a deep baritone voice. The couple had southern accents.

Ann overheard a discussion between Mr. and Mrs. Ferndale as they were hiking northbound.

Mrs. Ferndale spoke. "What was that man doing out here in the middle of nowhere? No backpack either."

Mr. Ferndale answered, "I don't know, dear. Maybe he lives somewhere nearby."

Ann also heard the lady mention something about trail blogs, but the voices trailed off as they moved farther away. It would be difficult to detect their proximity from where she stood. The trail was over a mile away and she didn't want to lose sight of their mission. It was getting late and they needed to find Peggy and Melody.

When they resumed their trek, she shared her thoughts. "Well, that was interesting. I could only hear a portion of the conversation. Apparently, the woman spotted a man without a backpack out here. If that's true, he might've been the one who shot your agent. Then the conversation quickly changed to discuss someone's blogs."

Steve was curious. "I'll check the *Trail Journals* site later. We are crunched for time right now."

*****

Mrs. Ferndale had been referring to blog posts created by *Bootlegger9*.

Bootlegger9 belonged to Samuel Regis, a part-time freelance computer programmer who loved the attention he received from a growing list of followers.

Early one morning, the group that Samuel had been paired up with for safety reasons decided to ditch him. They couldn't take all of the drama that seemed to surround him.

*****

Samuel was sitting alone on a decaying log, reading the latest headlines and checking the feedback from his blogs. When he heard something thrashing in the bushes, he quickly lifted his giant bald head to see what it was.

A lady with a disheveled appearance caught his attention. It looked like she had been crying and he couldn't help but see the blood stains.

Samuel hadn't immediately recognized who this person was. He was trying to be funny. "You all right over there? Were you attacked by a bear?"

Melody was not amused. She glared at him. She hadn't been in the mood for a chat. "No, I'm not all right. I need to find my sister. Have you seen a woman with auburn hair, about yay tall?" She used her free hand to mark her sister's height.

Samuel's chipper demeanor gave her an unsettling feeling. "Nope, you're the first person I've seen all day."

Then Samuel stood up and removed his sunglasses when he realized who he had been conversing with. "Wait, I know you! You're President Langford's daughter! MELODY!"

Melody nodded. She didn't like the way he blurted out her name. She quietly responded. "Yes, but would you please lower your voice? I really don't want the whole world knowing I'm out here."

"Oh, of course..." Samuel pretended to change his demeanor. Now he acted like he was a concerned model citizen. "I'd be glad to help you look for your sister."

Melody looked at the device he had been holding in his hand. "Thanks, but what I really need is a phone. Could I please borrow yours? My battery is dead."

"Sure, here ya go..." He swiftly handed her his phone.

Since she could only remember her mother's number, she dialed it. Instinct told her to turn away and speak softly into the mouthpiece to avoid being overheard. "I'm okay, but Peggy's missing. I've looked everywhere. I'm using someone else's phone right now." Melody was nodding her head. "Mmm, yes, I understand. In that case, I'm heading back now." Then she hung up the phone.

Melody handed the phone back. "Thank you, sir."

"Everything all right?" He wanted to get all the juicy details.

"Yes, thanks again. Gotta go…" Melody turned around and walked away.

Samuel shrugged his shoulders as he watched her disappear around the bend. *She sure left in a hurry. Wonder what that was all about?*

Moments later, Samuel accessed his blog page and resumed posting more inaccurate statements. *'Folks, you're never going to believe this, but I just shared my cell phone with Melody Langford, the President's daughter. She was out here hiking with her sister, Peggy, but now she is looking for her. All I could see was blood stains on Melody's clothing. It looks suspicious to me. I wouldn't be surprised if the Appalachian Trail murderer killed yet again.*

Stay tuned...' He felt it was his duty to make his personal blogs interesting.

Samuel had no filter. He never even tried to put himself in someone else's shoes. It was the thrill of attention he was after. He got some sort of high from posting about other people's low points.

*****

Agents Flex and Vern finally reached the location of the blinking dot. They found the scattered remnants of the broken satellite phone and some of Bixben's blood that had been left behind, but they did not find the President's daughters.

Agent Flex had been vigilant about keeping President Langford up to date on finding the girls. He immediately answered when his phone vibrated. "Yes, Madam President..." He listened intently. "Thank you. We'll wait for her here."

Agent Vern looked perplexed. "Did I hear that correctly? Her, meaning only one?"

"Yes, Melody should be here any minute. She has been in touch with her mother who urged her to turn around. Apparently, Peggy is missing."

Ann sighed. "That's not good, I wonder where Peggy could have gone. Hopefully she didn't run into the shooter."

"Got that right… We'll have to overnight here and get a fresh start in the morning. Hold on…" He paused to contact a friend and fellow Secret Service agent.

"Zack! I'm sending you the coordinates to bring the Opal home." *Opal* was the code name used by the Secret Service for Melody when President Langford was in office.

Secret Service Agent Zachary Wells responded, "Yes, sir, we are in transit now. We should be there in about fifteen…"

Flex replied, "Roger that."

While Steve waited, he used his phone to log onto the *Trail Journals* site to check out the latest posts. His demeanor changed when he read *Bootlegger9's* posts about the President's daughters. "What a complete idiot! Who does this guy think he is? He's putting the girls in danger by posting this shit!"

Agents Flex and Vern were relieved when Melody came into view.

Agent Flex's voice was stern. "Melody, there is a helicopter due to land here in about fifteen minutes. You need to return home. We will continue the search for Peggy and I will keep you posted on any new developments, all right?" More importantly, he needed to make sure Melody stayed out of harm's way.

*****

About an hour after Melody was rescued, FBI Agent Karen Daisy and CIA Agent Dave Zeller arrived carrying flashlights. They wanted to help Agents Flex and Vern search for the President's daughter.

It was pitch dark and they set up tents for the night.

Flex confirmed, "We'll head out early and canvass the area tomorrow."

*****

After a quick breakfast of granola bars, the team of four split up and searched the entire area.

FBI Agent Vern headed south and then west, looking for any signs of Peggy. Stubbing the front of her boot on a rock, Ann winced. Moving forward, she came to a fork. *Hmm, that way looks less cluttered, let's check it out.* Cautiously moving up the hill, the wind suddenly picked up, swirling a huge bunch of fallen leaves into the air. That's when Ann saw something out of place.

She cautiously walked over to the large piece of plywood that had been partially covered up with dirt and debris. She knelt down and brushed away large clumps of dirt and leaves. She felt something move. When she realized it was a large pivoting door of some sort, she gasped aloud. "What the...?" *This looks like some sort of animal trap! I'd hate to fall in there!*

That's when it hit her. *What if someone did fall in?*

Taking her mobile phone out of her back pocket, she tilted the door and used the flashlight feature to illuminate the darkness below. Seeing eyes peer back, Ann called down. "Peggy, please tell me it's you!"

Peggy shouted back, "Yes! Oh boy, am I glad to see you! I fell in here when I was trying to get a better signal."

Then Ann heard crumpling noises. *Footsteps!* She did not want to expose the President's daughter to a dangerous situation. She whispered to Peggy, "I just heard something… Wait here. I'll come back for you, okay?"

"Okay, no problem." Peggy had met Ann Vern once before. It was shortly after the attempt on her mother's life.

Several minutes later, Ann returned. "Peggy, I hate to do this, but I need to go check something out. I just want to make sure this area is secure before you come out, okay? It shouldn't take long."

*****

Ann followed the path back to the densely overgrown area she'd seen at the fork. Taking giant steps, she continued forward. She squatted down when she heard someone's voice. He had a Spanish accent. She believed it was a dialect from northern South America.

She froze when she heard a familiar voice. *Steve!*

Following the voices, she crept closer and closer. Her gun was now fixed in her right hand. She peered through the gaps in a stack of firewood and saw Steve Flex was tied to a tree. Only able to see the gunman's back side, she thought about how she would disarm him and free Steve. Just as Ann was about to pull the trigger, an unarmed heavyset fellow got in the way. *Dang it! Who are these people and what do they want with Steve?*

Unable to see the face of these men, she could only hear one of the voices. It sounded very familiar. *I've heard that voice before. I'm positive about it.*

When Ann saw the man's profile, she suddenly recognized who it was. *That's Mario Caesar! What's he doing out here?*

When Mario finally moved out of the way and she saw the profile of a much younger man pointing his handgun at Steve. Ann fired two shots. One maimed the gunman's hand and the other grazed Mario's arm.

Ramon immediately dropped the weapon. She quickly moved in and retrieved it. Then she pointed her gun at them. "FBI! Don't move! Put your hands in the air!"

With her free hand, she untied Agent Flex and kicked the gun that was knocked out of the young man's hands over to Steve. Agents Flex and Vern were now diagonally positioned, pointing their weapons at the pair.

Mario was whining about the pain, holding his bleeding arm. He begged for mercy. "Ahh! Please, please don't kill us!"

Agent Vern reprimanded him. "Look, if I wanted to kill you; you'd be dead already. It's just a flesh wound. You'll live."

Agent Flex suddenly recognized Ramon from the photos of the alert that he saw on his phone yesterday. But he didn't know how the Secretary of Homeland Security was involved.

Mario's breathing was intense. "You don't understand! Yes, Ramon and I were working together. But we had NO CHOICE! MALVADO has been holding threats over our heads!"

Agent Vern asked the next question, "I don't understand. Malvado?"

Before Mario could answer her question, another man with a thick Mexican accent grabbed Agent Vern from behind and used her to shield himself. His left forearm was tightly clenching her neck while his right hand pointed a pistol at her temple. "Drop the gun or you die." She immediately let go of the weapon.

Then the man nodded at Flex, "You too! Drop it now!"

Agent Flex placed the gun on the ground, stepped away, and lifted both hands in the air.

"Don't move! Ramon, tie him up! Don't try anything stup-"

Thwap!

Malvado fell forward, collapsing face down on the ground. His weapon discharged as he dropped to the ground.

Flex swooped in to scoot the gun from Malvado's hand. Now holding the gun on Malvado, Flex checked the man's vitals. "I'm not 100 percent certain, but I don't believe I feel a pulse."

When Ann finally turned around, she saw Peggy, covered in dirt, holding a tree branch. She had mustered the strength to climb out of the pit. Then she saw the perfect weapon just laying on the ground. Using all of her might, she swung it at Araña Malvado's head.

Once Agents Flex and Vern were properly rearmed, Mario pleaded with them. "Please, I promise, I'll tell you anything you want to know. I'll even tell you where Christine Welch's family is. They are safe! Malvado forced us to kidnap them in order to control what happened at the border."

Agents Flex and Vern exchanged glances in confusion. They were both unaware of the Secretary of Defense's missing family.

Ann asked, "I'm not following… What are you talking about?"

Mario confessed, "Malvado threatened to kill the Secretary of Defense's family. He was pure evil. He also threatened my family! I should never have accepted his political assistance when I first came to America. I was so naïve to think there wouldn't be any consequences. Look, I am truly sorry for my part in this whole mess."

Agent Flex wondered, "So what about those poor people on the Appalachian Trail? Are you telling us that Malvado forced the two of you to kill them?"

This accusation caused Mario and Ramon's heads to jerk back. The shocked look on their faces spoke volumes.

Ramon waved his hands in the air, "Whoa, whoa! Hold on, we never *keel* nobody. Only *keednap!*"

CIA Agent Zeller and FBI Agent Daisy caught up with Agents Flex and Vern. They arrived just in time to watch Ramon and Mario get handcuffed.

Agent Zeller spoke, "We heard the gunshots! What'd we miss?"

Agent Daisy looked at the body on the ground and scrunched her nose, "Is he dead?"

Agent Flex responded, "Well, let's just say, I didn't find a pulse."

Agent Daisy bent down to confirm. "Yup, definitely dead…"

Chapter 28 – Interrogation

FBI Special Agent Ann Vern finished watching the rest of the lengthy pipeline meeting, jotting down the names of those in attendance. She drew two columns, one group contained the names of those opposed to the pipeline. The other column contained those in favor of it.

She brought Martin Drawbuck in for questioning.

Agent Vern shoved a piece of paper with a list of dates in front of him. "Mr. Drawbuck, would you have a valid alibi for these dates?"

"I'm not talking without my lawyer present! I didn't do anything wrong!" Mr. Drawbuck repeated this response several more times.

Allowing him to place a phone call to his attorney, the FBI kept him in a holding cell.

Under his lawyer's supervision, Martin Drawbuck spoke, "Yeah, I was busy working on the pipeline."

Ann wanted proof. "I see. Can anyone confirm that?"

Martin tersely replied, "Look, we don't have time cards. I show up whenever the boss asks me to…"

Agent Vern did not have enough proof to hold him indefinitely. The attorney filed for his immediate release. "Fine, Mr. Drawbuck, you're free to go. Just don't leave the country."

After Martin Drawbuck was released, she sent Agent Flex a text. "I've come up with zilch. Drawbuck isn't saying much. He claims he was working on the pipeline."

Agent Flex arrived at the hospital. He wanted to check on Agent Carter Bixben's condition. As he was walking to the main elevator, he texted back, "Hang in there."

Chapter 29 – Hospital Visitor

As soon as Carter had been moved out of ICU, he was cleared to receive visitors. Melody just missed Agent Flex. She noticed a beautiful flower arrangement and decided to place a large box of Godiva chocolates next it. She fondly recalled how much Carter loved chocolate.

Melody sat on a recliner and glanced over at the monitors and IV lines connected to Carter's right arm. Every once in a while, she heard bleeps coming from the monitors. Then she studied Carter's features, thankful he was still alive. She reached out and folded his left hand in between her hands. Tears filled her eyes.

Carter's eyes opened. His voice was a little hoarse. "Melody, so glad you came to see me."

Melody spoke with tears in her eyes. "I've been so worried about you. How are you feeling?"

Carter winked at her, "You should know, you can't get rid of me that easily."

Melody smirked, "Is that so?" Then her demeanor became more solemn. "Carter, I don't know what I would do if anything ever happened to you."

Carter asked, "Would you really miss me?"

Melody blushed. "What kind of crazy question is that? Of course, I'd miss you."

Carter smiled. "Good! I'm glad to hear that! Say, how would you feel about going on a date with me after I get out of here? I mean we've officially known each other for more than eight years, but we've never technically gone out on a real date."

Melody was beaming. "I would love that!"

Chapter 30 – Isaad's Confession

While Emma Dil was reading young Taji his favorite super hero story, his father was tiptoeing upstairs to say good night. Taji sat straight up in bed, lightly patted his mother's wrist and asked, "Mommy, maybe Spiderman can capture that bad man."

Isaad stopped short in his tracks when he overheard his son's comment. It broke his heart when he realized how much it had affected him.

Emma replied, "Yes, Taji, that would be amazing." Then she cupped his little chin and looked into his eyes. "Listen to me, we are all safe now. Do you believe me?"

He nodded his head and rubbed his sleepy eyes. But when he saw his father poke his head in the doorway, Taji lit up. "Papa!"

"Did you read your favorite snake-man story?" His father loved to tease.

Giggling loudly, Taji corrected him, "It's Spiderman, Papa!"

Isaad smiled, "Oh, right! Did you remember to brush your teeth, young man?"

"Yes, Papa, I have mint breath now." Taji opened his mouth and huffed out.

"Very good, Taji…" Then Isaad patted his son's head. "Sleep well. School tomorrow."

Taji rolled onto his side and pulled the covers up around his face. His parents turned the light out and cracked the door.

*****

Downstairs, after Taji was fast asleep, Isaad spoke to Emma in their native language about the guilt he'd been carrying around ever since they arrived in the United States. "Emma, I will burst if I don't tell someone what I've been feeling in my gut. Abdul came here to hurt Americans. I'm certain of it. I would never forgive myself if something ever happened to our new home."

Emma squeezed his hand. "I understand, I think you want to be the hero in Taji's story."

Isaad squeezed her hand. "It is true, I've never been a coward before. Tomorrow we will go back to the base where our plane landed. I will tell them everything. If they find Abdul, maybe they can deport him."

*****

The next morning, after bringing Taji to school, his parents drove their 1992 Honda Accord to the entrance gate at Langley Air Force Base.

Rolling down the driver's side window by hand, Isaad showed the guard their Special Immigrant Visas. "Hello, I must speak to someone in charge. I have important information about possible terrorist."

The guard contacted his commanding officer. "Colonel, I have a man at the gate telling me he has information about a possible terrorist threat."

Isaad watched the guard nod his head and listened to him speak into the phone receiver, "Yes, sir!"

After the call ended, the guard pointed to an area just outside of the compound, off to the side of the road. "Sir, would you please park over there and wait for the colonel. He would like to meet with you."

Isaad answered, "Yes, of course. Thank you."

*****

Colonel Nome double checked the list of names for that particular date of arrival. There were several names beginning with Abdul. But there was only one person named Abdul Dil. Each refugee's photo had been taken before they were allowed to leave the base. Colonel Nome had an idea, "Isaad, perhaps you could point out his photo?"

Isaad nodded, "Yes." He spent more than an hour looking through the photos. Then he pointed his finger at one of the photographs. "There! That's him!"

The look of terror on his wife's face confirmed it. She shouted, "HEEE very bad man!"

Colonel Nome wanted to clarify, "You're absolutely sure?"

They feverishly nodded their heads in unison. Isaad spoke up. "Yes, that is him. You see, he use Dil so they think he was family."

Colonel Nome made a copy of the photograph and returned. "Mr. and Mrs. Dil, I completely understand why you couldn't reveal this information to us at that time. But I am certainly glad you have come forward today. If he is planning an attack on US soil, we definitely need to know about it."

Isaad Dil nodded his head. A huge burden was lifted from his conscience that day.

Colonel Nome contacted the Pentagon to relay information about a possible terrorist threat. Christine Welch at the Department of Defense received the information and shared it with the Secret Service, the FBI, the CIA, and Homeland Security.

Chapter 31 – Stockpile

Adam Pratt was tired of always picking up the slack for his coworker, Abdul. The man kept a scowl on his face, never speaking more than two words to him. The only time Adam witnessed him smiling was when he was kissing up to the boss. *Where does Abdul go during lunchtime? We are only allowed a half hour lunch, but he takes forty-five minutes or more.*

Working in the coal mine was a dirty, thankless job. After his mother died, his own father never even acknowledged the hard work Adam put in to pay the bills.

Adam felt like he was his father's care taker. Washing the dishes and cleaning up the mess while watching his dad in a drunken state of mind. He resented seeing the kids outside playing games. Secretly hoping he might one day return to being a child, he mopped the floor and grabbed a basket of dirty laundry.

His bicycle trip to the nearest laundromat required extra care and balance. On his route, he daydreamed about a better life.

Without warning, he swerved off the road. The laundry basket flew into the air and crashed on the sloping grassy swale, scattering clothes and towels everywhere. A pickup truck almost hit him. He thought the vehicle looked familiar. It had the same canvas tarp that was on Abdul's vehicle.

He gathered the laundry and rode the rest of the way to Thrifty's Laundromat. Instead of daydreaming, Adam chose to focus on how he was going to spy on Abdul. He needed to find out what Abdul was hiding. *I'm not covering his sorry ass any more!*

*****

Monday morning came around. Adam Pratt decided to set his alarm clock an hour earlier than his usual wake up time of 5:00 a.m. He made coffee the night before and poured it into a thermos, hiding it at the back of the chiller behind his brown bag lunch. He'd need the caffeine to wake up. It didn't really matter whether it was hot or cold.

*****

Adam was outside playing catch with his school friends. His mother was waving at him from the kitchen window. It was a beautiful day, without a cloud in the sky. But suddenly, the winds howled and sky turned charcoal. All of his friends ran away. Adam felt alone and scared. He watched helplessly as a tornado touched down in a field behind his childhood home in South Dakota. Sirens were blaring loudly. The noise just wouldn't stop. He covered his ears, but then sat straight up in bed, realizing it was his alarm clock going off.

Dreading the thought of getting out of bed, he contemplated resetting the alarm clock and falling back to sleep for another hour. *No, I need to find out what Abdul is hiding.*

Stumbling to the bathroom, he took care of business and changed into his work attire. After eating a banana and some dry cereal, he opened the door of the fridge and removed the thermos and his lunch and tucked it into his knapsack. He promised himself he would drink the coffee once he arrived at the mine.

On the bike ride to work, he thought about his mother and how she used to take care of him and his father. He remembered how she always made strawberry shortcake on Saturday nights and pancakes on Sunday mornings. Tears welled up, making it difficult to see. He stopped his bike and wiped a forearm across his eyes. He missed his mother. Then he pushed off and returned to pedaling.

Adam had been an only child, no siblings. It was difficult for Adam's father to pick up the pieces after the fatal accident. His mother's death was a pivotal moment when his dad began drowning his sorrows in alcohol.

*****

The headlight on Adam's bike was becoming dim. He knew it would soon need a new battery. Luckily, the light from a full moon helped him to be able to see. Coasting into the lot where

Abdul usually parked his truck, Adam stashed his bike in some nearby bushes.

Adam knew he would have to let Abdul think he arrived late to work. Contemplating his excuse, he decided to go with the 'I can't believe I overslept' bit. It felt weird to be here this early. He ducked out of the way, squatting next to his bike in the bushes. Making sure he was still able to see the parking lot, he opened his thermos and chugged the cold coffee which made him shiver.

*****

Ten minutes later, Abdul arrived in the same junky pickup truck with the tarp. Adam watched as he unzipped a couple of large suitcases. Then he rolled back the tarp over the truck bed and lowered the back gate. One by one, he loaded shiny metallic canisters into the luggage.

Hmm, I wonder what's inside those cans.

Glancing at his trusty glow-in-the-dark watch, Adam saw there was still an hour left before he was expected to show up for work.

Wait, what's this?

Adam watched as Abdul rolled the suitcases into the shadows, toward the elevator.

He must be going down into the mine. But why?

About a half hour later, Adam saw Abdul reemerge with the suitcases. Abdul repeated the process, pulling the tarp back and loading more canisters.

That's really strange!

It was close to the time when Adam usually arrived at work. Waiting until 6:00 a.m., Adam watched Abdul look around and then shrug his shoulders. Then Abdul entered the mine again.

Adam whispered to himself. "Okay, here it goes." He moved his bike back to where he usually parked. Then he collected his things and stepped into the cage, pressing the down arrow, the basket descended deep into the mine shaft.

About fifteen minutes later, Adam exited the contraption and made his way toward the area where a large coal seam was discovered. He and Abdul had been assigned to work in this section of the mine. The machinery and tools remained undisturbed, exactly where they left everything on Friday.

Adam wasn't the least bit surprised that Abdul was nowhere to be found. He didn't feel like talking to Abdul and decided not to speak at all. It wasn't like Abdul was his boss or anything.

When Abdul finally returned to do his share of the drilling, he never even looked at Adam.

Adam made up an excuse so he could exit the portal. He just said he wasn't feeling well and needed to get some fresh air. But Adam really wanted to find out what happened to the canisters.

Abdul seemed to accept the excuse, since Adam was never one to leave work early. "Don't take too long. The boss will be here any minute."

Adam nodded and slipped away. When he was completely out of sight, Adam picked up the pace, panting with all of his awkward gear on. When he arrived at what could only be described as an immense labyrinth, he did not know which chamber to take. Using his headlamp, he studied the ground and saw what he believed were fresh footprints leading into the far left tunnel. The tunnel plunged deeper and deeper, meandering left and right. Adam stepped over an old water pipe that had been used to flush out a portion of the mine after it was abandoned. He purposely stepped inside of each footprint to avoid creating a new set.

Adjusting his headlamp, Adam finally reached the end. Tilting his head down, he saw neat stacks of large coffee cans stockpiled against the old rock face. He swallowed hard, as he opened one of the canisters. He did not understand what he was seeing, so he pulled his phone out and snapped some photos. Then he returned the item exactly where he found it.

Moving as quickly as he could, he retraced the steps back to the tunnel's entrance, past the familiar cage elevator, and back to his work area.

But sure enough, the boss was waiting there with a scowl on his face. J. D. Mumpett, raised his voice, "Boy, where you been? Stop slacking off and get to work!"

Adam sheepishly looked at his feet. "Sorry, uh… yes, sir…"

The boss wasn't satisfied with Adam's answer. "I ain't payin' ya to do nothin'! Get that straight!"

Adam felt the heat creep up from the base of his neck. He just focused on his breathing. He could see Abdul's gloating eyes behind the mask.

*****

After his shift was over, Adam was exhausted. Waking at 4:00 in the morning had been rough on him. He wanted to just fall into bed and go to sleep, but he needed to stop someplace first.

Pulling his bicycle into the parking lot of the local police station, Adam lowered the kickstand and walked into the building. He asked the receptionist if he could speak to a police officer.

The receptionist studied him up and down and then asked, "What's this about, young man?"

"It's personal. Please, it's important. I really need to speak to a police officer, okay?"

Her mouth was making annoying snapping sounds as she chewed her gum. "Okay, but it might be a while. There's only one police officer here right now and he is on the phone."

"I'll wait, thank you." Adam sat down on a plush leather chair. After about twenty minutes, his head was bobbing. He tried to stay awake, but the day's events caught up with him and he drifted off.

He felt a tap on his shoulder and jumped up. "Whoa, hey there, I'm Officer Jones. Did you need to speak with me?"

Rubbing the back of his neck, Adam nodded his head.

"Well, come on back. We can chat in my office. Can I get you anything? A coffee or a donut maybe?"

Adam answered, "Okay, sure, thanks. That would be great. I'm starving."

Officer Jones set down the cup of coffee and a small paper plate with a glazed cruller. "What's your name, kid?"

"Uh, Adam..." He practically inhaled the sweet treat and gulped down the coffee.

"I can see you must've been hungry. What can I do for you, Adam?"

As the officer was taking a sip of soda, Adam just blurted out, "I think I took a photo of a bomb."

The officer immediately spit the beverage out. "Wait, surely, I must have misunderstood you. Perhaps you meant *photobombed*?"

"No, sir, I came here to report somebody at work. This guy, Abdul Dil, is bringing in large coffee cans and burying them deep in the mine."

Officer Jones was trying to process the information. "What makes you think it's a bomb?"

Adam replied, "I got up really early to spy on him. He was acting really weird. Then I followed him and watched him load a bunch of these coffee cans into suitcases and drag them into the mine. Here are the pictures I took. I only opened one can to see what was inside."

Officer Jones noticed the kid's naïve nature. "Excuse me for asking, but how old are you?"

Adam was already prepared with an answer to that question. "I'm nineteen. I need to work to help pay the bills."

Officer Jones was studying the photos on Adam's phone. "I see. Can you send me digital copies? I'd like to get this checked out."

"Sure!" Adam complied and sent the photos he'd taken of the canister's contents. Then he forwarded a short video clip. "I'm also sending you a video of Abdul. I took it inside the mine today, pretending to call my dad so he wouldn't be suspicious."

Officer Jones, cracked his door open. "Jackie, would you please give me the number of the FBI?"

Jackie responded, "Right away!"

Officer Jones initially spoke with Field Agent Rowe who patched the call to Agent Ann Vern.

*****

The photo and video recording was eventually shared with the Dils who confirmed it was the same man who'd threatened their son. Agent Vern immediately contacted nearby field agents, issuing immediate terrorist warnings.

Once the CIA, Department of Defense, Secret Service, and Acting Director of Homeland Security were made privy to this information; President Juniper was notified. The National Guard was deployed to protect this region and evacuate everyone within a large perimeter. Many feared the new pipeline's proximity to the mine might pose a problem.

*****

When the media got wind of the threat, reporters from every channel were lined up outside the surrounding military blockades.

Chapter 32 – The Note

When Mr. Mumpett learned about the mandatory evacuations, he offered to assist Adam and his family. Adam politely accepted. He shouted to his father, pleading with him to come with them. But Adam's dad blatantly refused to leave the premises. "I'm not going anywhere!"

Mr. Mumpett knew there wasn't any time to argue. "Adam, I'm sorry, but we need to leave now. The FBI has asked us for immediate assistance."

*****

Agents Vern and Flex rushed out to Beckley, West Virginia to meet with Adam Pratt and J. D. Mumpett. Just outside the secured perimeter, their helicopter hovered overhead before landing in an open field.

Mr. Mumpett and Adam stood watching the agents exit the aircraft.

After Agent Vern waved away the chopper, they rushed over to the pair. Ann didn't waste any time. She asked, "Where is Abdul now?"

Mumpett spoke, "I followed your instructions. Told him that Adam called in sick and I'd check back with him after lunch. The hidden cameras have been in place since last night. Looks like he's been working in the mine ever since five o'clock this morning."

"Mr. Mumpett, do you have that map we asked about?"

Mr. Mumpett unrolled an old map of the mine shaft and laid it out on the roof of his BMW. Adam Pratt immediately pointed to the area where he discovered the stacks of coffee cans.

Adam spoke anxiously, "It's right there!"

Mr. Mumpett placed a hand on top of his head. "But, I don't understand…. That section was abandoned and completely boarded up over twenty-some years ago!"

Adam interrupted, "The boards are gone now."

Agent Flex glanced at Agent Vern and then back at Mr. Mumpett. "Look, we are on borrowed time here! We need to come up with a way to stop this from happening."

*****

Meanwhile, fellow FBI agents surrounded the apartment that was being rented by Abdul Dil. Agent Jack Rowe shouted, "This is the FBI! Open the door!"

Kicking in the front door, Field Agents Jack Rowe and Ryan Luck searched for possible occupants. After releasing bomb sniffing dogs, they watched them frantically run around and then all three sat obediently next to the desk with a laptop computer and an open cardboard box.

A handwritten note was found inside, scribbled in English:

"This is an act of bravery for jihad. I sacrifice my life and will be awarded by Allah. Death to infidels and America! Abdul"

"Shit! It's happening!" Agent Rowe immediately phoned Agent Vern.

*****

Ann picked up her mobile phone. "Jack! What did you find?"

After listening, Ann exclaimed, "God help us!" After hanging up the phone, she looked at Agent Flex. "Big problem! It's happening today!"

Agent Flex was trying to maintain a calm composure. "Shit!"

Adam Pratt bravely stepped forward. "I might have an idea. When I was down there yesterday, I remember stepping over a large fire hose. Is there any way to flood the mine?"

Mr. Mumpett excitedly waved his hands in the air. "Of course! Adam, you're a genius!" He pointed to another area on the map. "You see this? Well, those gates are just above the area of concern. Two abandoned coal chambers full of trapped water and slurry were sealed off by two gates. It was done many years ago to prevent dangerous mine gases from building up over time. Two valves next to the parking lot control both Gates 5 and 6. You'll need to crank them open at the same time. Gravity will take care of the rest."

Agent Flex double checked, "Is anyone else down there?"

Mumpett answered, "No, just Abdul."

Agent Vern asked, "How long will it take to flood?"

Mr. Mumpett answered, "Seconds! It's really the quickest way."

Agent Vern commented, "We better hope Abdul doesn't have his finger on the detonator! Show us what we need to do."

J. D. Mumpett cautioned them. "The main valves are located just south of the cave's entrance, right here. But first, you'll have to remove the chains. Be sure to turn both counterclockwise at the same exact time." He popped open the trunk of his car and showed them a pair of bolt cutters. Then he tossed Agent Vern his keys. "Good luck!"

*****

As expected, the only vehicle in the parking lot was Abdul's truck.

Abdul had just finished unloading all of the explosives prior to their arrival. He was making his last trip down to the mine shaft in the elevator.

The detonator had been securely fastened to a large rock in front of the large stockpile. After his arrival in the chamber, Abdul kneeled down on his prayer mat. He bowed several times, facing in the direction of Mecca. The detonator was within his reach.

*****

The BMW was parked next to the pickup truck, which happened to be closest to the valves. Wielding a bolt cutter, Agent Flex dashed over to remove the links looped around each one.

Ann shouted, "On the count of three we start turning clockwise, okay? ONE, TWO, THREE!"

When they both tried cranking the old valves, nothing budged.

Steve was breathing heavy, "Shit, these things are rusted shut! We'll need some kind of lubricant!"

Ann pointed to the pickup truck "Steve, what about motor oil?"

Steve reached into the truck's open window and emptied the remaining contents of a plastic cup. Then he slid his lean body underneath the truck and removed the oil drain plug. He filled the cup with motor oil.

Ann retrieved the cup of lubricant from Steve and sprinted to the valves. She carefully poured the oil around both wheels.

Steve returned and grasped one of the metal wheels while Ann clutched the other. He panted, "On three! ONE, TWO, THREE..."

Chapter 33 – Flash Drive

Once Omar offered his condolences to Mrs. Archer, he returned to Ulysses's truck.

Ulysses just finished a conversation with his wife. She agreed that it was best to let Omar stay at their home until other arrangements could be made.

"Omar, if you're really worried about your safety, you're welcome to stay at our home for a couple of nights. My wife and I will help you find a more permanent place away from Merifrack, where you'll feel more comfortable."

Omar smacked his own head, mumbling to himself. "Of course! I just remember…back-up copy!"

"What? Where?" Ulysses couldn't believe what he was hearing.

Omar remembered exactly where he buried it. "In flower pot. We go to my apartment."

Ulysses thought about it. "I don't know if that's such a good idea. Somebody might see us lurking around."

Omar agreed, "Don't worry. We wait until dark."

*****

Later that evening, Ulysses drove Omar back to the apartment. Purposely parking away from any lighting, Ulysses turned the truck's headlights off. Leaving the engine idling, Ulysses whispered, "Okay, Omar, hurry up. I don't see anybody."

As soon as Omar opened the passenger door, Ulysses reached up and clicked the vehicle's interior auto lighting off. After the door was silently pressed closed, Omar vanished. It was difficult to see where he went, but that was the whole point. Ulysses felt his knees nervously twitching as he sat and waited. His gut kept telling him to get out of there.

*****

Omar crouched down, hidden in the shadows. When he reached the ceramic plant pot, he flipped it upside down and pocketed the soil-coated plastic bag holding the flash drive.

When he stood up, someone covered up his eyes from behind. Before Omar could react, a familiar voice spoke in Farsi. "Guess who…"

If he didn't have his guard up, Omar might have received the greeting better. His sudden defensiveness frightened Skid. "What the hell?"

Skid was wide eyed. "Hey, hey! It's me, all right? Take it easy! What's got you all keyed up?"

Omar waved his hands in a dismissive fashion and decided it was best to continue the conversation in Farsi. His voice sounded agitated. "Skid, don't take this the wrong way. What exactly are you doing here?"

"I came to see you, my friend. Although you don't seem very happy to see me." Skid looked hurt and confused.

Omar tried to compensate by patting Skid on the back. "I'm sorry. I've had a crazy week. Been going through a whole bunch of shit. Um…" He didn't have the heart to tell Skid that his timing sucked.

But before Omar could explain the situation, his attention turned toward a pickup truck with bright headlights peeling into the apartment complex, tires squealing. Omar was hyper alert. He sensed they were in danger and instinctively reacted. Dropping to the ground, he screamed, "Get down!"

Omar's head was under his arms. Bullets shattered the front windows and surrounding clay pots. Once the shooting subsided and the vehicle drove away, Omar slowly lifted his head to assess what just happened.

The glow of a nearby street light illuminated the front of his apartment which was now decorated with bullet holes. Then he looked down and saw a stream of blood. *No, no! Please no!*

Skid's upper torso had multiple bullet wounds. His eyes were wide open, but unresponsive. Omar shook the top of his shoulders, "Skid, Skid! Noooo!"

Omar did not have time to process his grief. His anger lingered. *Those bastards at Merifrack will pay for this!* There was no time to involve the police. It was clear someone wanted him dead.

*****

When he heard the shots, Ulysses dove down onto the floor of his truck. He feared the worst. *Please let Omar be okay…*

A loud tap on the passenger window startled Ulysses. But he was relieved when he realized who it was. "He reached up and unlocked the door."

"What the hell just happened?" Ulysses just wanted to get the heck out of dodge.

*****

Omar was out of breath. His head bobbed back and forth. It would be difficult to forget the bloody scene. "They kill… they kill my best friend! I should be dead!" He choked back tears.

"Na, na, don't you dare say that, Omar. It's not your fault! You hear me? None of this shit is your fault, dammit! We're getting out of this place."

*****

Arriving home late, Ulysses showed Omar to the spare bedroom. "We'll go to my office tomorrow. Right now, we just need to try and get some rest."

Ulysses was careful not to disturb his sleeping baby or his wife. Climbing into bed, it took a long while for his heart and head to calm down. But sometime in the middle of the night, he drifted off.

*****

At 6:30 a.m., Ulysses was startled awake by his baby girl crying. His wife was still asleep. He tiptoed to the baby's room and cradled his daughter in his arms. "I missed you, baby girl!"

After changing her diaper, Ulysses strapped a hands-free baby carrier around his shoulders and buckled it at the waist. Then he tucked baby Tiffany inside so he could safely prepare her formula. Gently bouncing her up and down, he cooed, "Are you hungry, sweetie? Well, it won't be much longer. Daddy's gonna feed you."

Mornings for baby Tiffany were usually better than evenings. The colic always seemed to begin at around 4:00 p.m. Smiling, Ulysses hummed the tune, *Rock a Bye Baby* while he fed and burped her. Not long after her feeding, Tiffany dozed off again.

*****

Eight o'clock rolled around. Mr. and Mrs. Drum were eating breakfast, reading the local newspaper.

When Ulysses saw Omar poke his head into the kitchen, he smiled. "Omar, you're up! I want you to meet my wife, Cynthia."

Omar shook her hand. "Nice to meet you."

Cynthia reciprocated the pleasantries. "Welcome to our home, Omar."

Ulysses realized that there wasn't any time for Omar to pack a bag. "Omar, I think I might have some things that will fit you. I kept all of my skinny clothes. Go ahead, take a nice long shower. I'll just place them on the dresser."

Cynthia was sipping coffee wearing a fluffy pink robe and matching slippers. She winked at Ulysses. "It was so nice of you to let me sleep in this morning."

Ulysses leaned forward and kissed his wife. "Figured you deserved a break. Omar and I are heading to the office later. It shouldn't take long."

Cynthia nodded once and grinned. "Mmm hmm… Hey, don't forget! I'm making your favorite dish tonight."

He winked at her. "Oh baby, I've already spent too many hours away from my girls. A pack of wild dogs couldn't stop me." He chuckled and leaned over, giving her a peck on the cheek.

When Omar returned, Ulysses stood up and grabbed a lightweight jacket and keys. "All right, Omar. You ready?"

Omar patted the left front pocket of a plaid flannel shirt containing the flash drive. "I think so."

*****

After arriving at the EPA office, Ulysses and Omar made their way toward Phil Houlton's office.

Ulysses whispered to Omar, "It's the last door on the left. Follow me."

Omar had to take twice as many steps to keep up with Ulysses. He couldn't wait to take down Merifrack, especially after what happened to Bill and Skid.

Ulysses could see Houlton's door was cracked open. He peeked through the gap and noticed that his boss was in the middle of an intense conversation. He turned to face Omar and placed an index finger to his lips.

Just before they walked away to give Mr. Houlton some privacy, Ulysses paused when he overheard his boss say:

"Look, calm down. I told you, it doesn't matter anymore. Merifrack has been cleared of any wrong doing. With Omar out of the picture and the evidence destroyed, it'll be smooth sailing from hereon out."

Ulysses looked at Omar with wide eyes. His mouth was open. He stood motionless, trying to absorb what he'd just heard. The only reoccurring thought was - *What the hell is going on?*

Omar tugged Ulysses's wrist to help him snap out of it.

They hurried, acting nonchalant in front of others at the office. Reaching a side door past the restrooms, they exited outside.

Ulysses was trying to catch his breath. "Truck… that way!"

The getaway vehicle was parked at the front entrance of the building. Ulysses felt his heart pounding. He was puffing, trying to keep up with Omar who was moving more quickly now.

When they rounded the corner, Ulysses was relieved to see no one lingering around on break. He didn't want to make up lies for any nosy coworkers.

Ulysses started the engine and drove to a deserted parking lot so he could pull his thoughts together. *Think! Think!* With the truck idling, Ulysses covered the top of his steering wheel with his forearms and lowered his head, closing his eyes. He could feel his blood pressure rising. *I'm going to have a heart attack right here!*

Several minutes later, he lifted his head. "All right, new plan! First, we need to go back to my house because I have to tell Cynthia what's going on. Then we will all go to the FBI headquarters in Washington DC. I'm probably being paranoid here, but we cannot trust our phones. They could be bugged. We can't take any unnecessary risks. As of now, Mr. Houlton is not aware that I know anything. We'll let the professionals handle it from here."

Omar was squeamish. "I dunno, I dunno… What if FBI won't help us?"

Ulysses tried to remain calm. "We need to try. I'm afraid we have no other options."

*****

Ulysses decided they would take his wife's minivan. It was already packed with baby essentials and they tossed in some more supplies and a couple of travel bags. Cynthia sat quietly in the front seat next to her husband.

She was staring out the front window, not knowing how to process what Ulysses told her.

The baby was fast asleep in the back seat next to Omar. The car's vibrations helped to soothe Tiffany.

As evening approached, they found a motel not far from the FBI building. Both rooms were put on Cynthia's credit card. Feeling that she needed to lie to the desk clerk, she added, "We are here for a family reunion and my cousin would like his own room please, but I want to pay for it."

The clerk answered, "As you wish, ma'am. Enjoy your stay with us."

Ulysses spotted a stack of business cards in a clear case. "May we please take one of your business cards?"

The phone at the reception desk began ringing. The clerk quickly responded to the question just before picking up the receiver, "Of course, help yourself." Then he answered the phone, "Good evening, thank you for calling *The Grand DC Hotel.*"

Omar helped the Drums carry their bags up to Room 415. His room was on the same floor, but several doors down on the opposite side of the corridor. Omar heard the little baby begin to fuss. He wished them a good night and added, "See you downstairs. Remember, breakfast at 6 a.m., dear cousin." Omar was trying to lighten the mood a little. It had been a long day and he could tell that they might be in for a longer night with their colicky baby.

When Omar scanned his key card and entered his quiet room, he relished the peacefulness.

Chapter 34 – Coal Mine's Chamber

Just as Abdul had been taught to pray in Arabic, he recited midday afternoon prayers while standing up. "Allah is the greatest." He kept his hands raised up next to his ears. Then he bowed. Prostrating himself in a *sajdah* position, he touched the prayer mat with his forehead and nose. Completely focused on praying, Abdul was oblivious to faint hissing noises overhead.

After praying, Abdul remained in a kneeling position. He wiped away what felt like a cold drip on his neck. Then he aimed a beam of light at the detonator and lifted the clear plastic lid, his thumb hovered over top of the silver button, preparing to press. He closed his eyes.

*****

Agents Flex and Vern hoped they would finally be able to move both valves after the cylindrical mechanisms had been covered in grease. Grasping tightly, they exhaled on the exertion as each applied tremendous effort to turn.

Steve grunted as he spoke, "It's moving! Keep… turning…"

Ann didn't flinch, her full concentration remained on the task. Hand over hand, she cranked the horizontally positioned wheel.

*****

With his eyes still closed, Abdul took a deep breath.

SWOOOOSH!

Engulfed in a sudden surge of cold polluted water, the rushing force caused Abdul to become separated from the detonator.

It carried Abdul down into another dark cave tube, twisting and turning. A whirlpool formed, dragging him under. He fought hard, trying to swim to the surface. It was difficult to determine the difference between up or down in the darkness.

*****

The earth rumbled and shook. As Agent Vern toppled backwards, she slapped both hands on the ground to avoid striking the back of her head. It was a technique she picked up from FBI training.

Agent Flex offered his hand and pulled Ann back to her feet.

Ann shouted, "Steve, what was that?"

He guessed, "It felt like a minor quake. Probably caused by a sudden change in pressure."

Ann shrugged her shoulders, "Possibly… One thing's for sure, they'll be sending in robots and drones to assess the situation."

Chapter 35 – FBI Interrogation Rooms

Ramon Blanco and Mario Caesar were placed in separate FBI interrogation rooms. Both men agreed to wave their legal rights to representation.

FBI agent Karen Daisy and CIA Agent Zeller recorded the confessions. They spent over four hours going back and forth to determine whether or not there were any inconsistencies.

Mario Caesar

Mario eventually disclosed where he'd been hiding the Defense Secretary's family. Just as Agent Zeller was getting ready to leave the interrogation room, Mario became emotional. "Please tell Christine I'm sorry. I never wanted any of this to happen."

Karen resumed the questioning.

Mario explained how Malvado threatened his family and his life. He'd been forced to comply with kidnapping instructions.

Karen recalled Mario pointing out a hidden tunnel to authorities. It was discovered at the southern border. "So why would you disclose the whereabouts of a tunnel that connected Mexico and Texas, especially if you were afraid of Malvado?"

Mario sat up and leaned forward, folding his hands on the table in front of him. "That's easy… You see, Malvado told me to do it. He had no interest in continuing to use an older route. He needed all of the attention shifted away from a new area that he was using to bring in more drugs, weapons, and people."

Karen filled in the blanks. "Let me guess, since you were the Director of Homeland Security, it would also appear like you were doing your job."

Mario answered, "Bingo! But there's more to this story. I need to tell you about OEYP."

Karen was curious. "I'm not following… What does OEYP have to do with this case?"

Mario told her all about OEYP (Our Empowered Youth Program, Inc.). "It was a fake 527 corporation acting as a legitimate business under a fake name, *Oscar Gordon*. But instead of helping troubled youth, it was a front for Malvado to park his money. Those funds were used for campaign contributions."

Karen remembered that name. When she sifted through her notes, she realized that Oscar Gordon was the mystery gentleman who sent flowers to Amanda Sky. "Would you know why Oscar Gordon would be sending flowers to Amanda Sky?"

Mario explained, "I remember that. Malvado liked to send pretty women flowers. And he bumped into Amanda when he was busy following Brent Volt. That was so he could send a message to the defense secretary."

Karen paused to stare at him for a few moments, eyes wide. "Wow!"

She resumed her questioning about the OEYP campaign contributions.

Mario explained how it worked. "You see, by bringing in illegal money, weapons, and cash to the United States, OEYP was able to contribute large sums of money to election campaigns, like President Juniper's." He paused to take a deep breath. "I'm not proud to admit this, but once President Juniper won the election, all OEYP needed to do was encourage him to appoint me as Secretary of Homeland Security. It was easy enough, considering my spotless reputation. It was all about keeping up with an illusion."

Karen asked, "Was President Juniper involved?"

"No! Hell, no! He believed this was a respectable corporation supporting his campaign."

That's when Karen left the room. "Wait here, I'll be back."

Ramon Blanco

Karen's expression remained neutral as she entered the other interrogation room. A notepad and pen were placed on the table at the opposite end of the room.

Ramon was fidgeting, his right knee was bouncing up and down. Whenever he was nervous, his English suffered. His explanation was in broken English. "Malvado *keeel* Delgado, mi amigo."

When he struggled to find the proper English terms, Karen suggested he speak in his native tongue. She was fluent in both English and Spanish.

Karen recorded his full confession, translating it to English. "I saw Malvado shoot at a man who stepped off the trail. He didn't want anyone near his hiding place. He even set a trap just in case."

*****

When Karen asked about the murders along the Appalachian Trail, neither Mario nor Ramon knew anything about them. Both detainees expressed how relieved they were to be free of the drug lord's threats.

284

*****

When it came to sentencing, the judge granted leniency to Mario and Ramon because they fully cooperated with the FBI. They also helped the military locate and destroy the new tunnels that Malvado had been using in trafficking operations at the southern border.

Chapter 36 – FBI Visitors

After showing the proper identification credentials and going through a rigorous security check, Ulysses and Omar were escorted to an empty office by a lady wearing a business suit and identification badge. After seating them, she instructed, "Wait here. Someone will be with you shortly."

Karen Daisy spent most of the previous night going back and forth between interrogation rooms. Her shift was almost over and she was reviewing her notes. There was a tap on her door. "Come in!"

The clerk spoke. "Two people just walked in from off the street, no appointments. They claim the matter is urgent and have requested to speak to an agent. Do you have time to meet with them?"

Karen's dark circles and lackluster appearance portrayed her exhaustion. "I suppose so. Where are they now?"

The clerk responded, "I sat them down in the auxiliary office."

Karen stood up. "Thanks, Audrey. I'll take it from here."

Karen walked into the room and greeted the men. "Could I bring you some coffee?" She was already holding a mugful. When they politely refused, Karen asked, "So what brings you to the FBI?"

Omar handed over the flash drive. His hands were shaking.

Ulysses provided some background information.

After sipping the hot brew, Karen rolled out a brown pleather chair and sat down. "So, let me get this straight. You overheard your boss, who happens to be the head of the EPA in Philadelphia, Pennsylvania, talking about killing someone?"

Ulysses confirmed, "Yes, ma'am! But we don't think Phil Houlton is working alone."

Agent Daisy tilted her head. "Are you sure you heard correctly? Help me understand why someone in his position would want Omar dead."

Omar explained in English, but fumbled it a little when nerves got in the way. "I work at Merifrack. But I help take pictures of violations and people are dead. They tie me up and want me dead too!"

Ulysses clarified, "You see, he has enough evidence on that flash drive to shut down Merifrack for good, but Houlton doesn't want that to happen."

"I see… Well, let's take a look, shall we?" Karen inserted the flash drive into her laptop. She carefully viewed each photo and the documents showing dates and times of each violation.

Ulysses leaned forward in his seat and whispered, "Look, my boss gave me instructions to locate those files on Merifrack. He paid for my motel room and demanded that I stay in town until I found Omar. At the time, I just assumed my boss's urgency coincided with his keenness in shutting Merifrack down. But the really strange part was when my boss ordered me to break into Omar's home."

That was when Karen looked up from her computer. "He did what?"

Ulysses was beginning to perspire now. He could feel his heart beating out of his chest, recalling what happened. "It's true! I believe Houlton wanted me to do whatever was necessary to get his hands on those files and Omar! Of course, I flat out told him I would keep looking for Omar, but I did NOT want to break any laws. When I knocked on Omar's door, the jamb was broken. I soon realized someone broke into Omar's apartment and gagged and tied him to a chair. He was right there in his living room!"

Karen immediately picked up the phone and requested Mr. Houlton's personal phone records for the past two years. "Let's see who your boss has been communicating with."

Omar cried out, "They kill Skid and Mr. Archer!"

Karen's eyes widened when he mentioned that name. Her colleague, Ann Vern, used to discuss some of the frustrating perplexities of the Appalachian Trail case she'd been working on. But Karen remembered the name *Archer*. She hoped it was still written on the dry erase board in a seldom-used conference room. "Excuse me, did you say, *Archer*, as in Bill Archer?"

Omar responded, "Yes, Bill Archer was a good friend. I was helping him get information on Merifrack."

"Wait right here!" Karen stormed out of the room and opened the door at the end of the hallway. She immediately took several photos of the marked up dry erase board with her phone. She used a nearby phone to call down to the records department. "I need to put a rush on that request for phone records!" *If it's true, how is Houlton connected to this and why?*

Karen returned to the office where Omar and Ulysses were sitting. She copied the information from the original flash drive and handed a copy to Omar. "Here, you now have a duplicate of everything you gave to me. We're going to need some time to figure this out. How will I be able to contact you? May I take your number?"

Ulysses exuberantly shook is head, "No can do, mm mmmm! I purposely left all of our cell phones at home. Don't trust them." He leaned forward again, but this time he nervously looked around before whispering, "Listen, my boss thinks I'm home sick with the flu. I sent him a text before we left town so he wouldn't get suspicious." He handed her a business card from the hotel. "This is where we are staying. I jotted the room number down on the back. My wife mentioned to the desk clerk that we were in town for a family reunion."

She scribbled a bunch of stuff on the back of her business card and handed it to Ulysses. "Okay, if you can think of anything else that might help us with this investigation, you can call my mobile number. I wrote the case number on the back. If, for some reason, you cannot get a hold of me; you'll have Special Agent Vern's information too."

Ulysses replied, "Yes, ma'am, I appreciate your help."

Agent Daisy offered some more advice. "One more thing… it's probably best to keep a low profile, at least for now. We'll keep in touch."

Chapter 37 – Searching

Drones and robots carefully scoured the coal mine after the chamber had been flooded. Every last canister was recovered along with pieces of the detonator.

Abdul's body was never found, despite multiple attempts. Eventually, the recovery crew called off the search. Reports determined it would be impossible for anyone to survive, given the circumstances.

*****

After exhausting all available resources, Christine Welch and her colleagues at the Pentagon were unable to locate her family. Believing that she needed to finally come clean with the President about what was going on, she drafted a letter of resignation.

She requested a private meeting with President Juniper. Her conscience would be clear. Threats made against her family and her coworker, Brent, needed to be disclosed. Christine was fully prepared to take the heat.

She hoped that by leaving her position at the Pentagon, she might be able to spare her family in the process.

When Christine entered the Oval Office, she couldn't believe it. Her entire family was standing there, completely unharmed. Speechless, she rushed over to hug each one.

President Juniper smiled, "We were briefed an hour ago about the circumstances involving the kidnapping. Mario Caesar apologized explaining that he'd been forced by Araña Malvado, the Mexican drug lord. You can thank CIA Special Agent Zeller, for bringing your family here today."

Agent Zeller adjusted his earpiece and nodded his head once.

Christine held her right hand over her heart. "Thank you Mr. Zeller! I am so grateful you found them. I'm in shock right now. I just can't believe Mario was involved!"

Then Christine turned toward President Juniper. "Mr. President, I was fully prepared to tell you everything. In fact, here is my letter of resignation. I'm sorry, I should have been more transparent with you about what was happening."

President Juniper took the letter and glanced at it. Then briefly looked up at Christine before he tore it into pieces.

Rip, rip...

As the remnants of her letter were drifting to the floor in the Oval Office, he firmly spoke. "I'm afraid I cannot accept this. Christine, I believe you were in a tough spot and acted accordingly. From this point forward, I'll need you to keep me apprised of all developments. Understood?"

"Yes, Sir, absolutely! Thank you."

"One more thing, I want you to take a week off and spend it with your family. That's an order..."

Chapter 38 – Return to DC

It was a long, quiet drive back to DC. Agents Flex and Vern didn't say much, clearly exhausted from the previous day's events.

When Steve dropped Ann off in front of her place, she spoke. "Steve, before you go, I just need to get something off my chest."

Steve was preparing himself for the worst. "Uh-oh! That doesn't sound good."

Ann's voice trembled. "Wait, hear me out first. Look, I really like you…"

Steve added, "I'm sensing there's a *but* clause coming."

Ann rolled her eyes at him. "The problem is I like you too much, Steve. I'm afraid of where our relationship is headed."

Steve smirked and raised an eyebrow, "Really? I thought, for a minute there, you were getting ready to dump me."

Ann finally built up the courage to say what she needed to say for a long time. "Steve, what I'm trying to say is…"

Suddenly, her mobile phone buzzed. It was Agent Daisy with a message alert in all caps. "Damn! Karen's calling, she never texts me in all caps. Must be extremely urgent. I need to go to the office."

Steve tilted her chin slightly upwards and kissed her on the lips. "I'd like to take you out on a proper date, whenever you're free. Then maybe we can finish where we left off, okay?"

She grinned and nodded her head. "Of course, that sounds wonderful. Get some rest. No need for both of us to lose sleep."

*****

Ann arrived at Karen's office. "What's going on? Your message sounded urgent."

Karen folded her hands and placed them on her desk. "You're not going to believe what we just uncovered."

Ann yawned and rubbed her eyes. "Karen, I haven't got a clue what you're talking about. You're going to have to enlighten me since I haven't had much sleep."

Karen responded, "I know what you mean. Look, before I head home, I need to tell you what recently happened. There was an interesting turn of events that could be linked to your Appalachian Trail murder case."

Ann perked up. "I'm all ears."

Karen showed her the statements that she recorded from Ulysses and Omar. Then she handed Ann the original flash drive, Phil Houlton's phone records, and all financial transactions linked to Phil's personal account.

Karen summed it up. "Phil is the director at the EPA in Pennsylvania. These guys overheard a peculiar conversation that involved a murder. You'll probably need some time to read it over. I might not have connected the dots if Omar hadn't mentioned Bill Archer's name. I'd seen that name many times before on the dry erase board in the conference room where I'd often eat my lunch."

*****

Ann returned to her office and read through the statements. She hoped this was the Appalachian Trail murder connection she'd been looking for. She gathered the pile of evidence containing victims and suspects and lugged the files into the conference room. She focused on phone records, date ranges, and financial information.

A few things caught her immediate attention, like the number of phone calls made between Phil Houlton and Martin Drawbuck. Then she located financial transactions for Houlton and Drawbuck. Apparently, they received large sums of money from OEYP. That was the same fake corporation owned by Araña Malvado.

Ann was fitting more pieces together. *Hmm, what do we have here?* According to another report, Houlton held large amounts of stock in energy producing oil and gas corporations. More importantly, he heavily invested in

299

Merifrack and Valley Wing Pipeline. Phil Houlton would lose a shitload of money if those businesses ever went under.

The financial deposits made to Drawbuck coincided with the estimated date ranges of murders found along the Appalachian Trail. The first deposit into Drawbuck's account was made shortly after the first meeting that Arthur Brown attended.

Ann folded her arms in front of her. *That is no coincidence! He was murdered after he provided expert testimony against the pipeline.* According to her notes on the case, hikers discovered Arthur Brown's dead body not long afterwards.

*****

Agent Ann Vern wanted to solidify this case. She didn't need anyone getting away with the murders because of loopholes. She reviewed what the ranger in Harpers Ferry sent her.

She hollered, "Hallelujah! Well, isn't that convenient!"

After matching all of the nicknames with the victims', Ann noticed they all had something else in common. They not only fought hard against pollution, but they volunteered. They all maintained various sections of the Appalachian Trail within approximately 100 miles of Harpers Ferry.

She left a message. "Steve, when you get this message, call me back."

As she was typing up a formal report, her phone vibrated. His photo appeared. "Steve! Do you think you can swing by my office. You're not gonna believe what else I found."

"Sure, can't wait!"

Chapter 39 – State of the Union

Members of Congress and guests were gathered at the Capitol. Cameras were rolling and members of the press were speculating about what might be included in President Juniper's State of the Union Address.

The Sergeant at Arms stepped forward and announced, "Madam Speaker, the President of the United States!" The United States Marine Band played *Hail to the Chief.*

President Bradley Juniper entered the room, smiling and waving. He shook hands with nearby colleagues and friends. Before he could reach the podium, he was immediately stopped by Leonard Higgins who spoke directly into the President's ear.

President Juniper nodded in agreement. Then he proceeded to the space behind the podium and shook hands with Vice President Vince Ackroy and Charlene Jones, the Speaker of the House.

The clapping and cheering died down.

President Juniper waved his hand. "Thank you. Before I begin, the president of the NAACP mentioned that he needed to make an announcement. So without further ado, Mr. Leonard Higgins, you have the floor."

"Thank you, Mr. President, I promise to keep this brief." Leonard adjusted the position of his head so he could speak directly to the President of the United States. "Sir, I'd like to personally apologize for allowing untrue statements and accusations to tarnish your reputation. Clearly, you have honorably demonstrated fairness toward all Americans. On behalf of the NAACP, I am truly sorry for any impropriety."

President Juniper nodded his head. They shook hands and Mr. Higgins returned to his seat.

President Juniper covered many topics. The economy was strong under his leadership so when he finished the update, he received a standing ovation.

He continued, "It is my duty, as your President, to abide by the law, to admit when something is wrong, and to do my best to fix what is broken. I recently became aware of lies and coverups associated with a non-profit organization that was supposed to be fostering programs to empower and protect our youth. I knew something needed to be done to prevent organized crime from operating under fake corporations. I have decided to appoint a dear trusted friend to lead a committee of experts to pinpoint and dissolve illegitimate businesses. Please give a warm welcome to Navy Lieutenant and your former President of the United States, Robin Langford."

President Langford stood up, waved and smiled.

Everyone stood up and clapped.

President Juniper waited for the clapping to subside. "Furthermore, there are several people here tonight who I'd like to personally thank for making our country safer. Thanks to the dedication of Ann Vern and Karen Daisy from the FBI, Steve Flex from the Secret Service, and

Dave Zeller from the CIA who ultimately formed an alliance, going after drug cartels in Mexico. Our Nation's safety is one of my top priorities." He shifted back from the microphone and paused.

Waves of clapping and hooting echoed loudly in the chamber.

President Juniper adjusted the mike. "Nobody knew that when Agents Flex and Vern began their search for the Appalachian Trail murderer, it would lead them to political corruption. Thanks to their perseverance, the responsible parties are now being held accountable."

More clapping and hooting were heard.

"While on a hiking expedition, these sisters heard gunshots, but instead of running away, they turned back and saved the life of a Secret Service agent. Agent Bixben wouldn't be with us tonight, if it hadn't been for the heroic actions of Melody and Peggy Langford. Thank you." President Juniper paused to clap.

Secret Service Agent Bixben was emotional. He stood up, walked over to Peggy and Melody and hugged each one.

Another round of applause…

"Ahh, but that's not all… You see, Peggy Langford accidentally stumbled into a trap when she was trying to find cell service. Instead of waiting to be rescued, she figured a way out. But that's not all, Peggy's fearless act of bravery helped to take down the malicious kingpin of a Mexican drug cartel, thereby saving the lives of FBI Agent Ann Vern and Secret Service Agent Steve Flex who were being held at gunpoint."

Peggy was still standing up next to her sister. She graciously smiled and waved a hand.

There was more thunderous clapping from the audience.

The President continued, "I'd like to thank a man who did not turn a blind eye to the corruption in his department. He worked as an inspector for the EPA and discovered that his boss was destroying documentation necessary to completely shut down a fracking operation in Pennsylvania. This individual was able to completely shut down a fracking corporation responsible for allowing toxic waste to seep into a lake that was set aside for drinking water. And if it weren't for Mr. Drum bringing this matter to the FBI's attention, we never would have discovered who was responsible for the gruesome Appalachian Trail murders. Ulysses Drum, would you please stand up? Mr. Drum is now the new EPA Director for the Mid-Atlantic region."

Ulysses stood up and smiled, holding a miraculously peaceful baby in his arms. His wife, Cynthia, was at his side.

Audience members were whistling, cheering and clapping...

"Ah, but Ulysses wasn't alone. He had the help of a refugee from Afghanistan who risked his own life to help a community protect its drinking water supplies. Omar Qurban helped Ulysses and the EPA gather enough proof to permanently shut down Merifrack. To show our appreciation, Members of Congress and I would like to issue Omar a proclamation granting him honorary citizenship in the United States."

Omar stood up, smiled, and waved. He'd previously been granted a temporary visa.

The crowd applauded loudly.

President Juniper pressed his hands on either side of the podium. "I'd like to recognize a few more heroes tonight. Without their prompt intervention, we might have had a different outcome."

President Juniper looked out at the audience. "You see, a member of the Taliban threatened an Afghan's family to gain access into the United States during the evacuation process. When Isaad Dil notified military personnel about the breach, the Department of Defense, FBI and CIA were quickly corralled to try and find him. The trail ran cold until a young fellow by the name of Adam Pratt, stepped forward. He complained to local police about a coworker's suspicious activities. When the name and photographs of this person fit the profile that

Isaad provided, agents resumed their search for the perpetrator.

Adam Pratt's prompt action helped the United States thwart a terrorist attack. Bomb recovery crews found the remnants of a detonator and large stockpiles of explosives. Pyrotechnical experts confirmed it would have been forceful enough to cause massive destruction and loss of lives. We are so very grateful. Please stand up, Isaad Dil and Adam Pratt."

The heroes received a standing ovation and lengthy applause.

Chapter 40 – Date Night

Steve Flex rented a tuxedo for a romantic night out with Ann. He slicked his hair straight back for a more sophisticated look. After he slapped on some aftershave, he checked his image in the mirror and adjusted the bow tie. He suddenly felt the urge to mimic a popular Ian Fleming character, with a perfect British accent. "Flex,… Steve Flex… I'll have a martini; shaken, not stirred."

Just before he was supposed to arrive at Ann's place, he visited a flower shop and picked out a bouquet of red roses mixed with white lilies.

Steve couldn't help but notice how unbelievably gorgeous Ann looked in a sleeveless emerald gown with a plunging V neck. "Ann, you always know how to take my breath away." He smiled and blushed a little when he handed her the beautiful arrangement.

Steve booked a private table with a view at one of the swankiest restaurants in DC. He wanted this evening to be perfect.

The waiter brought some menus and presented the evening's specials. Then he disappeared to give the couple time to make a decision.

Conversation was easy. The respect and trust had always been there. It was difficult to deny that their formidable alliance had blossomed into something more.

When the waiter returned to take their orders, Steve asked for their finest bottle of wine, the waiter nodded and replied, "Good choice, sir."

Minutes later, a sommelier arrived and poured just enough for Steve to taste. After approving, two wine glasses were promptly filled. The rest of the bottle was placed in a nearby ice bucket to chill.

Steve reached across the table and gently grasped Ann's hand. "Ever since I met you, we've had a special connection. I feel like you are the perfect mate for me."

Ann felt the gentle warmth of Steve's hand. She studied his features and saw how the candlelight danced in his eyes. "Oh, Steve, I've never felt this way about anyone EVER. You're right, we do share a special bond."

Steve caressed her hand before reaching into his left side pocket. "I think it's time I showed you how much I love you." Then he slowly opened a tiny black velvet box.

Ann reacted by placing both hands on her rosy cheeks. Her eyes widened. "Steve! It's beautiful!"

Steve immediately dropped down on one knee and asked, "Ann, will you marry me?"

Ann grabbed onto his strong broad shoulders and looked him straight in the eyes. "Steve, I've fallen in love with you too! I hope you know that. Marriage is not something I want to rush into. You know, I've always been an extremely independent woman in complete control of my life. This is all happening so quickly. Please understand, I'm not saying *no*. I just need you to give me some more time. I hope you understand."

Steve returned the boxed item to his coat pocket. Then he stood up and kissed her on the forehead before returning to his seat. "Ann, your independence is one of the many things that I love about you. Of course, I understand. You're worth waiting for. And you're absolutely right, there is no need to rush into anything."

Ann exhaled. "Thank you. I love you, Steve Flex."

Steve leaned over and they passionately kissed. His voice was a little hoarse, "I've never felt like this before. I love you, Ann Vern."

Chapter 41 – Unfinished Business

After their dinner date, Agents Flex and Vern had a bone to pick with someone. What they really wanted to do was teach that person a lesson.

Ann Vern giggled as she dangled a paper in front of Steve's face. It was a copy of the trail nicknames the ranger had given to her. *Bootlegger9* was highlighted in yellow. "You're never going to believe what I found out about this guy. Do you remember the visit we made to the Appalachian Trail Conservancy in Harpers Ferry? The ranger told us they hired a computer tech guy."

Flex squinted his eyes. "Yes, I do remember that. What about it?"

"I kept calling and leaving messages, but he never returned any of my calls. But that doesn't matter. Well, Samuel Regis uses the trail name *Bootlegger9*."

Agent Flex grasped it from her hand and logged onto the *Trail Journals* site. "No way! You're kidding!"

Bootlegger9 had been posting more lies. His latest blog read, *'Hey, everyone, I decided to head back home. The trail was way too overgrown. There is no way I want to risk getting injured.'* The fact of the matter was that Samuel's two weeks of vacation were up and he needed to return to the real world.

Steve shook his head in disgust. "This guy is full of excuses! He sounds like a bonafide wimp, if you ask me. How about we pay him an official visit and scare the crap out of him? After all, he did put Melody and Peggy in danger by posting about them."

Ann was doubled over laughing. "Steve, we have to play this by the book. It's true, but we need to take this seriously."

Agent Flex cleared his voice. "Okay, okay, I know you're right."

*****

Knocking on Samuel's door, it was around 9:30 p.m. They heard a gruff man's voice shouting, "I'm coming! Hold your horses!"

Agents Flex and Vern exchanged glances just before the door opened.

"What's this all about? I'm in the middle of my dinner, in case you didn't know!" Samuel Regis sounded perturbed.

They flashed their badges and told him they needed to take him in for questioning concerning an FBI matter.

Samuel shooed his hand. "No way, is this some sort of joke? I don't find it the least bit funny! Look, my hot dogs are getting cold, so if you don't mind..."

Agent Vern pulled out her handcuffs and read him his rights. "Sir, this is no joke. You've been ignoring my calls and so now I must take you down to FBI headquarters for interrogation. We have some serious questions about your recent trail blogs. If you fully cooperate, you'll be able to return home." She slipped the cuffs around his wrists.

They were walking to her car when Steve spoke. "I'd be nice to the FBI agent if I were you, Mr. Regis. You wouldn't want to be on her bad side."

Samuel's eyes widened.

Steve winked at Ann as he sat down in the front passenger seat.

Samuel was wiggling in the back seat, mumbling in agitation. Then he blurted out, "I have rights, you know! I want my lawyer!"

Agent Flex turned around. "Listen, sir, I don't think you realize. Serious charges have been brought up against you for putting the President's daughters in danger. We have copies of your blogs on *Trail Journals*. Now, it could take a while to locate an attorney for you. We just have a few simple questions to ask you. So why not cooperate? I'm pretty sure you wouldn't want to spend the night in a holding cell while we wait around for an attorney to show up. But that's totally your decision."

Samuel looked down and sheepishly shook his head. "Look, let's just get this over with. I have nothing to hide."

"Good, all you need to do is tell her what she needs to know and we'll bring you back home. Simple as that,... understood?"

Samuel nodded his head.

*****

In Interrogation Room Number 3, Samuel Regis sat down.

FBI Agent Vern asked if he wanted a cup of coffee before they began. He refused. "No, coffee gives me the runs."

Ann purposely did not look at Steve, afraid she might burst out laughing at this point. She read Samuel his rights again and clarified, "You do have the right to an attorney, Mr. Regis. You're welcome to wait here until we can locate

318

one." Ann sensed he wanted to get this over with.

Samuel was nervously breathing rapidly, "No, I'll answer your damn questions."

"All right, then we will proceed. Mr. Regis, were you aware that by blogging about sensitive information on a public website, it could have put President Langford's daughters at risk?"

Samuel answered, "What? No, I never meant to hurt anybody!"

Agent Flex added, "Sir, your personal trail blogs have been taken down at this time because we have reason to believe it might have contributed to a Secret Service agent being shot."

Samuel's hands were trembling. His bladder was becoming uncomfortable. He almost forgot he wasn't wearing his *Depends*. "No, no! I swear, I was just telling stories. I didn't think it was a big deal. If I knew it would have caused all of this, I would never have posted about it."

He was squirming in his chair. "May I please use the bathroom?"

Ann unlocked the cuffs. "Certainly, Agent Flex will accompany you."

When the agents felt that Samuel had been through enough, they brought him back to his home.

*****

After dropping Samuel off, Ann asked, "Steve, do you really think we got through to him?"

Steve shrugged his shoulders. "Who knows? He seemed more concerned about abandoning his hot dogs. We can only hope someone like that will think twice before putting sensitive things on social media websites. But if history's any indication, he'll be complaining about the hot dog company next."

Ann could not contain her laughter. After catching her breath, she added, "Oh, I suppose you're right, Steve. *Oscar Mayer* will have to handle it from here."

Chapter 42 – Steve's Discovery

Steve had been busy tying up loose ends concerning the Appalachian Trail murders. He was working with computer specialists in the field to find out more about the ranger's computer that was hacked in Harpers Ferry.

Steve met up with Ann Vern.

"Steve, I can hear the exhilaration in your voice. What is it?"

Steve grinned before admitting, "Guess what, my team was finally able to pinpoint the exact date of when the ranger's computer was hacked."

"Really? Wow, okay, then when?"

After blurting out the date, she double checked the pipeline public meeting date and noticed the hack happened almost exactly one week after the meeting. "Wow, that cannot be a coincidence, Steve!"

"Yes, and with Ranger Flip's help, we were able to retrace the computer's keystrokes. Funny thing, the volunteer sign in sheets were always accessed on Mr. Flip's days off. It was during the time when Samuel Regis had been hired to fix the bugs and install security updates."

"Jeez! Does that mean what I think it means?"

"Wait that's not all. The bad guys made another huge mistake…"

Steve removed a manila envelope that had been tucked inside his jacket. He slid out blown up photographs containing images taken by nearby CCTV cameras at various locations. "These are stills from the video footage. Did you happen to notice who was chatting with Phil Houlton? I seriously doubt there's food in that bag."

Ann placed both hands on top of her head. "Holy *Oscar Mayer* wiener! It's SAMUEL REGIS!"

*****

Samuel Regis was immediately arrested and taken into custody where he finally admitted being paid by Phil Houlton to access computer records that contained the full names of the volunteers who were murdered. He was sentenced to 30 years for being an accessory to murder.

Epilogue

Security was tight, temporarily blocking public access to the Supreme Court. A grand occasion was being held here. Secret Service agents were strategically placed. Only a couple of news crews were invited to capture the event.

Sixteen marble Corinthian columns majestically supported the West Pediment of the Supreme Court building. In the outdoor Oval Plaza, a gathering of close family and friends were perched on white linen covered chairs. It was a picture perfect autumn day. Violinists dressed in long royal blue gowns played soothing music. Large ornate vases adorned the steps leading up to the front entrance.

Stuart James Marker, Chief Justice of the Supreme Court, was dressed in formal court attire, holding a Bible. Standing to his left was the groom-to-be, Carter Bixben and his best man, Steve Flex.

Carter was wearing a Calvin Klein charcoal gray tuxedo with a boutonniere consisting of Miniflora white roses and Opal Phlox.

Peggy, the maid of honor, gracefully glided down the aisle as onlookers stood by. She was wearing a designer gown created by the world famous Rochelle Ivy. It was an elegant teal gown with long, peek-a-boo sleeves and pearls adorning a high neckline. The top portion of Peggy's long auburn hair was tied back with matching ribbons, tiny pearls and baby's breath. She held a bouquet containing Dwarf Sunflowers, Shasta Daisies, and Opal Phlox.

Then the violins shifted abruptly to a staccato rhythm as they played the *Wedding March*. The guests stood up and turned around, waiting to see the bride.

Melody Langford was a stunning sight. It was another Rochelle Ivy masterpiece designed specifically for her. The cream colored Victorian inspired gown with its antique lace train was studded with tiny white opals. It was dazzling. Her highlighted hair was in a marvelous updo and she wore a simple see-through veil. The oval backless dress with long flowing satin sleeves and intricately sewn antique lace dress panels just barely showed her low-heeled pointy pumps covered in crocheted lace. She held a gorgeous cascading bouquet of off-white Hybrid Tea Roses, Baby's Breath, Opal Phlox, and Shasta Daisies.

Robin Langford, mother of the bride, wore a beautiful navy blue crushed velvet gown. She was standing next to her mother, her eyes were misty with joy for her youngest daughter.

Cheryl Huff, Melody's grandmother, kept dabbing her eyes with a handkerchief. She wore an emerald green formal dress suit.

Melody and Carter were officially married by the Chief Justice of the Supreme Court that afternoon. The outdoor ceremony could not have been more perfect.

A reception was held inside the Supreme Court's basketball court on the fifth floor. President Juniper made an appearance and properly made a toast to the bride and groom, wishing them well.

Special Thanks

Thanks to my family for providing me with encouragement to fulfill my dreams.

Stephen and Alex, you never cease to amaze me. Keep up the good work. Your perseverance is admirable. Despite life's curve balls, you both remain steadfast and demonstrate leadership, courage, and resilience.

To my husband, Joe, thanks for supporting my writing journey. Your patience is appreciated whenever I need to detach and focus.

Special thanks to Ley Errico, my special friend. I love our unexpected adventures, whether it's tea and a chin wag in the afternoon or coming up with our own answers to the latest *Ann Landers'* columns. We will always have each other's backs no matter what situations arise. It's fun contemplating future characters and story lines too.

Janet Steadham, I'm grateful for our friendship. Thanks for all of those brilliant suggestions, and your support and guidance. I admire your dedication in whatever you put your mind to.

Rita and Craig Rodekurt, your friendship means so much. I enjoy our get-togethers. Thanks for your encouragement and taking the time to read and critique my books.

Debbie and Karen Windhorst, forever friends that I will treasure forever. Thanks for sticking by me throughout the years.

Note from Sheri McLaughlin:

When the pandemic caused us to retreat into isolation, it helped me to discover a new passion: writing fiction books. I'm humbly grateful to be able to share fun stories with others. Imagination has taken me on a wonderful journey, and I'm thankful to be able to embrace this whole experience.

Thanks for giving me a chance to grow as an author.

If you have enjoyed *Mercy on the Trail*, I do hope you would consider leaving a review. Thank you.

Author Website Information:

For information about purchasing additional books written by Sheri McLaughlin, along with newsletters and updates, please visit the author's official website.

www.sherimclaughlinauthor.com

Or scan this QR code:

Categorized Index

Grant Pearl - Melody's college boyfriend and former fiancé who had been hiding a secret gay lover

Bill Harper - Vice President of the United States under President Robin Langford

Kelly Farrah - An extreme liberal Democrat who ran for President against Bradley Juniper

Bradley Juniper - Moderate Republican from Atlanta, Georgia; becomes President. Civil Engineer and former CEO of an engineering firm

Nancy Roy - Secretary of State under Bradley Juniper

Alicia - female US Marine who came to the aid of two Afghan women

Gary Delta - an international news anchor

Amy - international reporter

Deborah Wooly - Secretary of Homeland Security under Robin Langford's Presidency; expressed concerns about national security.

Frank Wilson - President Juniper's Chief of Staff

Harold Kowolski - President Juniper's Press Secretary

Mario Caesar - President Juniper's Director of Homeland Security who works with the Secretary of Defense. Put in charge of security issues at the border.

Brenda - President Juniper's aide who works closely with the Secret Service to help arrange last minute trips

Polly Arnold - The only Democrat on President Juniper's team. She sets up meetings.

Leonard Higgins - President of the NAACP

<u>**Supreme Court:**</u>

Stuart James Marker - Chief Justice of the Supreme Court who swore in both President Langford and President Juniper

<u>**Afghanistan:**</u>

Isaad Dil - Afghan refugee who helped United States intelligence before needing to evacuate his homeland. His son, Taji, was threatened by Abdul (Taliban). Married to his wife, Emma.

Emma Dil - Afghan refugee who fled Afghanistan with her husband, Isaad, and son, Taji.

Taji Dil - Young Afghan son of Emma and Isaad who was threatened by Abdul (member of the Taliban). Loves his favorite super hero, Spiderman.

Abdul - Taliban soldier who takes the last name 'Dil' by threatening a boy named Taji so he could gain access into the United States

Alibaba "Ali" Finjaven - discovered his mother and sister had been killed by the Taliban. Sent a coded alert to his father. Afghan refugee who fled to the US (Texas). He was accepted at Texas A & M University

Rammi Finjaven - Ali's father, was detained by members of the Taliban and then released. He carried a fake passport so the enemy would not find out that he worked as a translator for the United States. The Taliban killed his wife and daughter. He fled Afghanistan with his only son and they settled in a small suburb near El Paso, Texas where he works as a mechanic at El Paso International Airport.

Anqa - Ali's little sister

Ikram - Ali's neighbor and best friend in Afghanistan.

Omar Qurban - worked in the construction business in Kabul, Afghan refugee transported to a military base in Virginia. Lost contact with his friend, Skid, during the evacuation process. Understands and speaks the Pashto language and Farsi. He also learned how to speak English. Received a temporary visa when his passport was confiscated by the Taliban. Met Bill Archer and agreed to work and spy on Merifrack.

Skid Nuri - Afghan refugee with few teeth. Found his parents dead in Kabul. He became close friends of Omar and worked for a medical supply company. During evacuation process, he lost touch with Omar when he was transported to Randolph Air Force Base. Carried a work I.D. badge because the Taliban confiscated his passport. He speaks the Pashto language and Farsi and only knows limited English. He was granted a temporary visa and sought employment at a local shipyard in San Antonio, Texas. He hoped to reconnect with his buddy, Omar.

Hazrat Aryo - Taliban leader in Afghanistan

Rodney - an American soldier stationed at a military base in Wisconsin. He interviewed Skid Nuri in Farsi

Mexican Border:

Delgado - Refugee and friend of Ramon's who joined a group of fellow Venezuelans to travel to the Mexican border. He spoke up when a drug lord wanted more money.

Ramon Blanco - Venezuelan refugee who was Delgado's friend and partner. Joined a group of Venezuelans to enter into the United States through the Reynosa, Mexico. Is forced to help Araña Malvado when he is short on cash. Invited to stay with Rammi and Ali.

Araña Malvado - tall, dangerous bearded man; drug lord of Mexican cartel in Reynosa. He is heavily armed. Trafficking drugs, weapons, and people across the Mexican border.

American Citizens:

Amanda Sky - Brent Volt's girlfriend held at gunpoint by a man with a ski mask.

Brent Volt - lives in Baltimore. Commutes to Washington DC (Pentagon) to work for DOD. His boss is Christine Welch. Is threatened by a masked gunman.

Roxy - waitress at the *Chug it Down* bar and grill in Williamsport, Pennsylvania. Only works on Mondays and Wednesdays.

Ginger - chubby waitress at the *Chug it Down* bar and grill in Williamsport, Pennsylvania. Works part time from Thursday through Sunday.

Rochelle Ivy - World famous designer who makes gowns for the President's daughters.

Cheryl Huff - Robin Langford's mom and Peggy and Melody's grandmother

<u>United States Security Detail</u>:

Steve Flex - Secret Service Agent and Navy Seal, who worked with the FBI to bring down those responsible for the assassination attempt on Robin's life. Most of his teammates call him "Flex". He hiked the Appalachian Trail using the name, "Iron Jack" after his tour ended in Afghanistan. Has a crush on an FBI agent.

Ann Vern - a feisty red-headed FBI Special Agent who enlisted the help of Secret Service Agent Steve

Flex. She help bring down those responsible for the assassination attempt on Robin's life. Reconnects with Steve Flex at Maxi's Diner.

Karen Daisy - oftentimes works with her friend and colleague, Ann Vern. She was reassigned to a case in El Paso, Texas.

Dave Zeller - CIA Agent working closely with the FBI when international intelligence sources obtain new information.

Zachary Wells - "Zack" Secret Service Agent

Jack Rowe - FBI Field Agent

Deputy Director Edward Phloeb - Works in Washington DC and issues assignments to Secret Service personnel.

Carter Bixben - Secret Service Agent and Navy Seal in charge of keeping the Langford sisters safe on their Appalachian Trail journey.

Ryan Luck - FBI Field Agent

Christine Welch - President Juniper's Secretary of Defense who works at the Pentagon. She soon discovers her family has been kidnapped.

General George Whitlock - works with the President and the Secretary of Defense at the Pentagon

Coal Mine:

Adam Pratt - was born in South Dakota. He lost his mother in a tragic car accident. Lives in a small wooden shack with his alcoholic father. He dropped out of school so he could work in a coal mine. He is only14 years old, but must lie about his age.

Abdul Dil - works at the coal mine with Adam

Mr. Pratt - Adam's father who cannot hold down a job because of his drinking problem. He reads day-old newspapers and complains about everything.

J. D. Mumpett - Adam and Abdul's difficult boss at the coal mine.

Officer Jones - Helps Adam Pratt

Jackie - Gum chewing receptionist at the Police Station who first meets Adam Pratt.

Hiking the Appalachian Trail:

Glenn Flip - Ranger at Harpers Ferry

Margaret - Young girl who works at the Appalachian Trail Conservancy at Harpers Ferry.

Mr. & Mrs. Ferndale - married couple who was sleeping in a tent in West Virginia along the Appalachian Trail and experienced an earthquake.

Samuel Regis - He is an elderly gentleman who works part-time as a freelance computer programmer. An attention-seeking hiker on the Appalachian Trail, nicknamed *Bootlegger9*, with a big mouth, complains about everything. He blogs about stuff on social media and the website, *Trail Journals*.

Mark Spieler - Hiker on the Appalachian Trail. Friend of Norman Conrad. Felt the earthquake in Pennsylvania while crossing a boulder field

Norman Conrad - Hiker on the Appalachian Trail. Friend of Mark Spieler. Felt the earthquake in Pennsylvania while crossing a boulder field. He has a deep southern accent.

Fracking and Pipeline:

Morton Hendrix - Amateur mechanic who worked at his father's garage; former UFC fighter. Lost most of his hair and wore a toupee; his grandfather left him a fracking business in a Will & Testament.

(He is the new owner of Merifrack, Inc. and voted Republican so the fracking business could start up again.) Inexperience caused major disruptions and visits from the EPA.

Bill Archer - retired attorney from Virginia and member of the RATC (Roanoke Appalachian Trail Club). He moved to Williamsport, PA and became an advocate for locals fighting for clean water. Makes public complaints about Merifrack. Also requests expert opinion from Professor Brown against construction of the pipeline.

Connie Archer - Bill Archer's wife

Dr. Gregory Terrance, Jr. - President of West Virginia University. Helps Agents Flex and Vern.

Valley Wing Pipeline - (VWP) Construction company installing a new natural gas pipeline.

Martin Drawbuck - VWP Construction Supervisor. He defends the construction of the pipeline.

Merifrack, Inc. - a fracking corporation owned by Morton Hendrix. It receives several violations and is discovered polluting nearby watersheds in Pennsylvania.

Ulysses Drum - Married man and a new father, His baby's name is Tiffany. Works as an inspector at the

EPA Division in Region #3. He focuses on fracking violations in Pennsylvania and West Virginia.

Phil Houlton - director of the EPA in Mid-Atlantic Region #3. Works out of the Philadelphia, PA office and is Ulysses Drum's boss

Cynthia Drum - Ulysses Drum's wife and Tiffany's exhausted mother.

Tiffany Drum - Drums' newborn baby girl with colic

<u>Murder Victims on the Trail</u>:

Arthur Brown - first victim discovered by hikers on the Appalachian Trail. He was a college professor with a PhD in Geology and Earth Science. Agrees to help Bill Archer by providing information about the proposed pipeline. His nickname was "Brown Bear" on the *Trail Journals* website. Lived in West Virginia.

Mark Wickham - Appalachian Trail hiker found dead. He was an attorney and a Democrat who lived in West Virginia. His hiking nickname was "Turtle Man".

Catie Minnow - Appalachian Trail hiker found dead. She was a Democrat and a software engineer nicknamed "Meta Key".

William Roy Taginaw - Appalachian Trail hiker found dead. He was a geologist and a Democrat who was nicknamed "Tagging Out". Lived in Virginia.

Jim Dennis - Appalachian Trail hiker found dead. He was married without children and a Republican. His trail nickname was "Lego Man" because he liked building things with Legos. He was a pastor and friends with William Taginaw.

<u>Agencies and Acronyms</u>:

OEYP - (Our Empowered Youth Program, Inc.) - a 527 tax-exempt corporation that allows contributions to campaign contributions. It was set up to foster programs empowering and protecting children and young adults.

SSSN - (Safe Social Sponsoring Network) - an emergency program set up under the Juniper Administration to handle work incentives for migrant workers crossing the southern border

RATC - (Roanoke Appalachian Trail Club)

PREVIEW – QUANTUM MERCY

Release Date: August 18, 2023

(Book #3 in *Mercy Trilogy*)

QUANTUM MERCY

Reanimating the Dead

Sheri McLaughlin

Preface

While writing Quantum Mercy, I drew from one real life experience that I will never forget. About 29 years ago, I needed to have a deviated septum repaired. I was only breathing out of one nostril. It had been time to see an otolaryngologist.

I'd always suspected that my nose had been broken at some point during my childhood. You see, I was a late-bloomer when it came to athletics. My hand-eye coordination, as a child, was not very good. I'd been struck in the face and nose more times than I'd care to remember, mostly by stray balls.

The doctor left me with the impression that this corrective surgery was routine and minor. I agreed to have the procedure done.

As they prepped me for surgery, I remember chatting with nurses, fixing my gaze on their faces to avoid seeing the IV needle go into my arm. A short while later, someone mentioned they would give me something to relax. I fell asleep moments later. I would later learn that the cocktail consisted of mostly Valium.

During surgery, I woke up, fully alert, lying flat on a stiff operating table. The horrific fact was I could not open my eyes, move, or speak. I felt trapped in my own body. This was not a dream, but it felt like a nightmare. I overheard a conversation between my doctor and his medical team. It sounded like he was lecturing a group of medical students.

Suddenly, my focus shifted to the warm pressure and sharp chiseling pain. Physically unable to move, I kept trying to think of another way to grab someone's attention. As my nose was being packed with gauze, tears pooled in the corners of my eyes. Alas, I heard a female voice say, 'She's awake!' I was so relieved. I thanked God for activating my tear ducts.

The surgery turned into a three-hour ordeal. I would later discover that the complication involved the bridge of my nose. It had been broken in three separate places.

*****

I've always had a healthy curiosity for scientific phenomena. During the research phase of *Quantum Mercy*, I became obsessed with the topic of cryonics. There were so many intriguing things that scientists have discovered. There is still much to be learned. But I do think it will be possible to reanimate a dead person someday.

Prologue

Immediately after graduating high school, Dorothy Brach and Robin Huff joined the Navy. That's where they first met each other. They were recruits in boot camp at the Great Lakes Naval Training Center. The training facility was located in Illinois, near the western shore of Lake Michigan. It was a brutal and rigorous process, but Robin and Dorothy remained determined to fight through the pain and exhaustion. Eventually, they excelled and overcame weaknesses, while leaning on each other for encouragement.

Dorothy Brach was a bright student who kept thoughts to herself, most of the time. She had a thirst for traveling abroad and a zest for learning to speak a new language. Dorothy earned a bachelor's degree in Russian Language and Literature, becoming fluent. After serving in the Navy for four years, Dorothy worked as a Russian translator for the CIA.

Robin Huff earned her college degree in Political Science while serving in the Navy for seven years. Her dedication paid off. At the age of 24, she was promoted to Navy Lieutenant and served for another eight years. When she came home on vacations, she often made arrangements to visit her friend, Dorothy.

Robin met Gerry Langford when she was 31 years old. Gerry had been twelve years older than she was. Robin had been working as an aide for a Senator from Wisconsin. She met Gerry at the Capitol. Gerry had been the Senator of Maryland, at that time. Although their party affiliations were different, they shared similar views and concerns. They were married six months later.

Robin left the military shortly after becoming pregnant with her first daughter, Peggy.

After Robin gave birth to Melody, Dorothy became pregnant with Lucy. When their kids were young, they would schedule play dates. Dorothy was called 'Aunt Dorothy' by Peggy and Melody. Lucy just called Robin 'Auntie'.

Lucy Brach spoke Russian well. Ever since she was a child, her mother spoke to her in both English and Russian. It was beneficial, as few Americans could speak Russian. Lucy also earned a bachelor's degree in Russian Language and Literature. One week after Lucy's college graduation, her mother died of a massive heart attack. The shock was devastating. She didn't know what she was going to do with her life.

Robin was there for Lucy, giving her the support she needed. She even helped Lucy look for employment using the language skills she had.

Like her mother, Lucy wanted to work for the CIA. She took special courses and, eventually, obtained a high clearance level. She worked as an operative in the counterterrorism division while living and working in Russia. Under a fake Russian passport, Lucy used the name Demitrivka Volkov.

Gerry was a senator for 12 years before being elected as President of the United States. After he was diagnosed with Parkinson's Disease, Gerry tried different trial drugs to manage symptoms. Unfortunately, he had a bad reaction to one of the medications and became hospitalized. His staff had no choice but to invoke the 25th Amendment, removing him from office just before the election. That election would make history, as the results were unprecedented. Robin Langford was sworn in as President of the United States at the age of 57.

Robin Langford had been recovering in the hospital after the assassination attempt. Lucy was granted special permission to take a two-week leave of absence so she could visit her auntie.

Gerry supported Robin's decision to run for another term. He was proud of his wife.

Robin had been on Air Force One, en route to California, when she received the shocking news about her husband's death. Gerry Langford died from a blood clot in the brain, a complication of Parkinson's disease. Robin's world had been turned upside down.

Robin Langford made a difficult choice to do what was best for the country she loved. She dropped out of the election. Robin decided to back Bradley Juniper, the Republican nominee.

Chapter 1 – Run on the Beach

Peggy Langford finished a five-mile mid-morning jog along Fort Lauderdale beach in scorching 90-degree heat. She was wearing a dark pair of sunglasses and a Marlin's baseball cap. As she neared the parking area just outside of the Yankee Clipper Hotel, she spotted her rental car.

Checking her pulse, she noticed a large black SUV with tinted windows slowly circling the lot.

Hmm, bet they'll want my space. After wiping her brow and eyelids with the left sleeve of her turquoise t-shirt, she reached into a belly bag and retrieved a set of keys. Crossing the lot, she unlocked the driver's door and slid inside. Closing the door behind, she started up the ignition and blasted the A/C. Waiting for the warm blowing air to become colder, she plugged in her mobile device to recharge. Even though it still had 35% left, she didn't want to let the power dwindle too low.

Looking in the rearview mirror, the same SUV spotted earlier was sitting idle directly behind, blocking her in. Mumbling to herself, "What a moron! Jeez, if you want this spot, you're going to have to give me more room to back out."

While she waited, she reached behind her seat and removed the lid from a small styrofoam cooler. Grabbing one of the chilled electrolyte replacement beverages, she twisted the orange lid and chugged it down. She only paused to wipe her face with a checkered towel that was folded in the passenger seat. Checking the rearview mirror again, the same vehicle hadn't moved.

What a jackass! Can't they see I'm trying to leave? Maybe they're texting or something.

Several more minutes passed. The heat caused Peggy's impatience level to boil over. She exited the vehicle and walked toward the rental's rear bumper, waving her hands at the SUV. The tinted windows were so dark, she was unable to see inside. She hoped her motioning would get the point across and coax the obstruction out of her way.

Unexpectedly, a hefty man with long, dark wavy hair and a dark tan stepped out of the passenger side. He was wearing dark sunglasses, a white button-down shirt and a pair of dark brown Bermuda shorts. Multiple gold chains surrounded his neck.

The hair on the back of Peggy's neck stood straight up. She backed away. When she saw the man move toward her, she rushed back into her rental. Before she could close the door, a large meaty hand grabbed her left wrist. She screamed and tried to pull away, but not before a needle plunged into her arm. Dizziness and confusion preceded the loss of muscle control. Peggy's head fell forward, striking the steering wheel, sounding the horn.

*****

Peggy awoke mid-flight during a discussion on board a private jet. She felt the small plane's abrupt movement during several minutes of unbridled turbulence. The plane changed altitude and, eventually, the shaking subsided.

The drugs in her system disallowed Peggy to move, open her eyes, or even speak. She felt like she was trapped in the twilight zone. The smell of new leather filled her nostrils while her face pressed against the seat back. A tightly secured strap around her waist created a sharp tug whenever the plane bounced.

Unrecognizable voices speaking in American English altered her focus. With a fully alert mind, she eavesdropped on the conversation.

A man with a deep southern accent spoke softly to another man. Peggy could only discern part of it. "… POTUS ever finds out, it's prison time for all of us."

The other guy's voice was scratchy but much easier to understand. Amidst labored breathing, he spoke with occasional bouts of coughing. "Ya gotta relax, eh? All security cameras were disabled. Nobody saw anything. The boss needs us to deliver the subject and then we're home free. We've gotta just keep our cool for another couple of hours."

There were no other names mentioned. These people seemed much more concerned about the President finding out. The reason for the abduction was not obvious. Peggy's mind looped around the possibilities. A dull ache crept from the base of her neck and moved toward the top of her skull. The pulsing pain synced with every heartbeat.

Chapter 2 – Cryonics Lab

Lab technicians dressed in full white plastic suits and head shields were monitoring the chambers' temperatures. Three years were spent working on regrowing neural circuits using stem cells. Twelve deceased corpses were preserved, administered cryoprotectants within minutes of death.

This project was experimental and remained strictly classified. Not even President Juniper was aware of the progress. Experimental and risky, the person who originally authorized it was dead. Controversial details have been kept under lock and key ever since.

Professor Damian Reid was selected as the head of Project F-12. Deep in concentration, he studied the reaction of frozen stem cells on AC-9, the ninth antifreeze concoction developed for the purpose of reanimating the dead after vitrification. He needed to correct dysfunctions in the brain matter, forcing the connections to bypass heavily damaged neural circuits. He was on the cusp of a scientific breakthrough. If he was right, it would become a game changer in the medical field. The professor overlooked many safety protocols, hoping to prove his theory would work. He was running out of money and needed to persuade the government to fully fund cryonics research. Sheer stubbornness and the thought of conquering death pushed the professor forward.

*****

The private jet landed in a dusty barren airfield. After coming to a complete stop, the engines were turned off and a ramp was lowered. Two husky men wearing Army pants and white t-shirts moved Peggy onto a firm flat stretcher. An IV had been inserted into her right arm just prior to landing.

Semi-conscious, Peggy felt the drugs wearing off. The change in temperature and dry dusty air caused her eyes to water as a warm breeze entered the cabin. Nobody noticed as they were too busy maneuvering the stretcher.

A small group of medical personnel were standing under a large awning attached to an insulated aluminum building. When one of the nurses noticed teardrops forming in the corners of Peggy's closed eyes, she exclaimed, "Hurry along! She's waking up!"

*****

Professor Reid preferred working in the lab alone, without any distractions or obtrusive interruptions. His abilities bordered on the genius level. That required absolute concentration. Even the most subtle noises would set his temper off. Sometimes he would walk around the complex with noise cancelling headphones. Another quirky habit involved rechecking the temperatures of the stainless steel holding tanks, or chambers. It was almost as if he expected them to suddenly change. The tanks held steady at -273° C (-460° F), which was a temperature he used to preserve human organs, slowing down molecular activity.

The Russian-born professor was in his mid-fifties. He was formerly known as Vlad Czechi in his home country, changing his name fifteen years ago when he defected to the United States. He never married. His flat personality and stoic demeanor contrasted against his wild medium-length salt and pepper hair, now parted on the left. The wavy locks just barely touched his slavic cheekbones. His icy light gray eyes were unexpectedly soft, almost calming. His Russian accent was the only thing that gave away his heritage. Professor Reid spoke English well.

The professor was a bit paranoid. He had always been afraid of what might happen should his research ever end up in the wrong hands.

www.ingramcontent.com/pod-product-compliance
Lightning Source LLC
Chambersburg PA
CBHW051732250726
48659CB00001B/27